Brimming with creative inspiration, how-to
projects, and useful information to enrich your
everyday life, quarto.com is a favorite destination
for those pursuing their interests and passions.

First Published in 2022 by The Harvard Common Press, an imprint of The Quarto Group,
100 Cummings Center, Suite 265-D, Beverly, MA 01915, USA.
T (978) 282-9590 F (978) 283-2742 Quarto.com

The Harvard Common Press titles are also available at discount for retail, wholesale, promotional, and
bulk purchase. For details, contact the Special Sales Manager by email at specialsales@quarto.com or
by mail at The Quarto Group, Attn: Special Sales Manager, 100 Cummings Center, Suite 265-D, Beverly,
MA 01915, USA.

26 25 24 23 22   1 2 3 4 5

ISBN: 978-0-7603-7418-4

Digital edition published in 2022
eISBN: 978-0-7603-7419-1

Library of Congress Cataloging-in-Publication Data
Names: Szymanski, Kris, author. | Kalkraut, Slawek, author.
Title: Men with the pot cookbook : delicious grilled meats and forest feasts / Kris Szymanski & Slawek
   Kalkraut.
Description: Beverly, MA : The Harvard Common Press, an imprint of The Quarto Group, 2022. | Includes
   index. | Summary: "From mouthwatering steak to captivating forest and fire photos, online sensation
   Men with the Pot bring their unique recipes, techniques, and bushcraft to the page with the Men with
   the Pot Cookbook"-- Provided by publisher.
Identifiers: LCCN 2021055420 (print) | LCCN 2021055421 (ebook) | ISBN 9780760374184 (hardcover) |
   ISBN 9780760374191 (digital)
Subjects: LCSH: Outdoor cooking. | Barbecuing. | LCGFT: Cookbooks.
Classification: LCC TX823 .S996 2022 (print) | LCC TX823 (ebook) | DDC 641.5/78--dc23/
   eng/20211214
LC record available at https://lccn.loc.gov/2021055420
LC ebook record available at https://lccn.loc.gov/2021055421

Cover Design: Tanya R Jacobson
Page Design/Layout: Amy Sly
Photography: Menwiththepot, except Adam DeTour on back cover and pages 1, 16, and 201

Printed in China

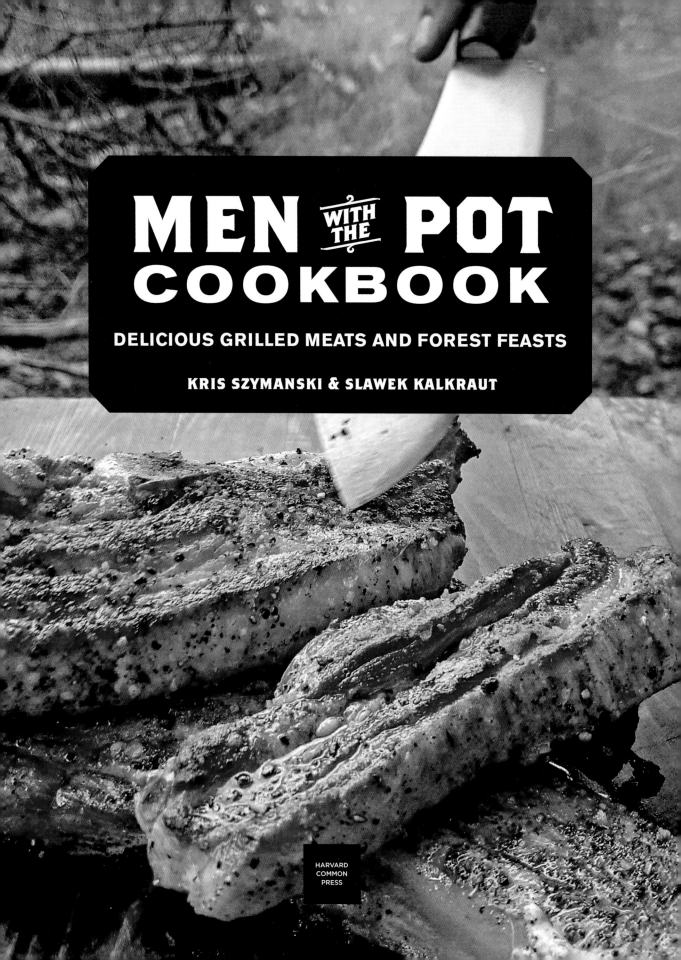

MEN WITH THE POT COOKBOOK

DELICIOUS GRILLED MEATS AND FOREST FEASTS

KRIS SZYMANSKI & SLAWEK KALKRAUT

HARVARD
COMMON
PRESS

CONTENTS

INTRODUCTION
Welcome to the Forest

Hello! *Witajcie!* We are Slawek and Krzysztof, two Polish friends living in Northern Ireland. In our ten years of friendship, we've bonded over a mutual love of braving the elements to create mouthwatering meals.

Maybe you're already familiar with *MenWithThePot* from Instagram, TikTok, or YouTube. What started as an Instagram page, where we shared our outdoor creations with friends and family, quickly snowballed into a passion project that people all over the world began to connect with.

Folks often ask us why our videos have caught on the way they have. From the beginning, we decided we should offer something different. On nearly every social media cooking channel, it's all about the cook or the chef, and there's always a person's face in front of you sharing a childhood story. We realized we were tired of the people cooking the recipes—we wanted to see the food! For us, it's all about food and nature, especially the beautiful sounds of both.

At that time, we did know about ASMR (autonomous sensory meridian response, that blissful tingling sensation you get with certain soothing sounds or visuals), but that wasn't our original goal with the videos. Then, as we searched through social media, we happened upon a woman on YouTube, and there was just something about her we couldn't pinpoint— she was just talking! But something about her voice wound its way into our ears, and that idea became the basis of what we do. (Except for that time loggers started working with saws beside us; they completely destroyed the whole ASMR thing . . .)

Going back to that first video, we figured we'd set out into the woods because we've both hunted and fished, and we've both cooked lots of dishes before. The first recipe we made was ribs. We used a cast-iron pressure cooker, added potatoes, onion, and a bunch of spices, and cooked it for 2 hours—in a firepit we put on an island in a stream! We didn't know what we were doing! In fact, if you scroll down to our first recipes on Instagram, you'll wonder, *What are these guys doing?* But you can also see progress—we're getting better! Those ribs, by the way, were falling off the bone and *very* good.

By viewer request, we now have a cookbook. If you've been following our videos, here you'll find many of the recipes. We hope you'll enjoy them as they were meant to be—out in the woods—but you *can* re-create them at home. If you're new to us or you've been camping before, you might be used to a certain kind of camp food. This isn't that! There's no hot dog on a stick here. Because we believe in eating tasty, *real* food—we prep and assemble everything on site.

We've been in this forest so long that we've given up trying to find our way out! Cooking delicious food is something we'll be doing forever. If you do what you love, you don't work a day. And if you can pay the rent and provide a good life for your family, why not do it? When we started with social media, nobody thought it would be possible to keep it going—and we don't know what the future will bring—but everything is going all right today. So, next time you're wandering through the woods, take a sniff . . . you might just catch a whiff of our latest creation wafting through the wilderness!

Happy cooking,

Slawek and Krzysztof

A FIELD GUIDE

FOR USING

THIS BOOK

If it isn't already obvious, we would much rather spend our days out in the forest than shopping for ingredients. And we want that for you, too. We frequently use whatever we happen to have on hand, and the recipes still turn out great! Food should be fun, after all, so don't stress the small stuff. We do, however, have some tips and suggestions that will help make your time in the woods more successful.

TOOLS

If you've seen just a couple of our videos, you know we enjoy making many of our tools. But we can't make everything! Here are some things we use frequently:

BOWLS: Two large bowls (same size) for mixing, serving, and covering and a small or medium bowl for mixing.

CAST-IRON POT (5-QUART, OR 4.5-LITER): If you'll be cooking over the fire the way we do, you'll want one with a hanging handle, rather than something like a Dutch oven.

CAST-IRON SKILLETS (2 [12-INCH, OR 30 CM]), WELL-SEASONED: Cast iron is unbeatable for cooking, especially with fire. Don't use anything coated with enamel (unless you don't mind ruining the enamel).

ENAMEL OR STEEL CAMP CUPS (2 large [12- or 16-ounce, or 360 or 480 ml]) with a handle (or small saucepan with a flameproof handle).

FLINT: It's how we start our fires (see How to Light Your Fire, page 19).

GRILL PANS (2, SAME SIZE): Ours are 11 inches (27 cm) with handles on either side but use whatever you have (so long as the handles are flameproof).

HANDSAW: Helpful in bushcrafting.

HATCHET: Useful for chopping firewood; we also use the blunt head as a mallet.

HEAVY-DUTY OVEN MITT: Something leather, like a barbecue or welder's glove, not what you use in the kitchen, so you're not burned by the high heat.

KNIVES: Large chef's knife. One rainy day, when we were unable to cook outdoors, we decided to make a knife. We went into a shed and came out a few hours later with what would become our most-asked-about tool: our signature 7½-inch (19 cm) cleaver. For us, it's a universal instrument that chops, slices, stirs, flips . . . whatever we need. Plus, a smaller (6-inch, or 15 cm) camp knife: We often use this for whittling.

LARGE CUTTING BOARD: Our wooden one is 11 × 18 inches (28 × 45 cm), and we frequently roll dough to "the size of our board." We actually have two boards, one dedicated for cutting proteins on.

MEASURING SPOONS (see Forest Hack, at right): Yep, for measuring.

MORTAR AND PESTLE: It sounds strange, but everything tastes better when made with a mortar and pestle; we don't know why, it just does—but feel free to use a food processor for chopping, crushing, or mixing ingredients.

PARCHMENT PAPER: To help prevent foods from sticking to the cooking vessel and to make cleanup easier.

PASTRY BRUSH: For brushing on sauces, melted butter, glazes, etc.

ROLLING PIN: for rolling doughs.

SKEWERS: We whittle our own (see Make Your Own Skewers and Holder, page 68), but you can use wooden or metal ones if you prefer.

SPIDER OR SLOTTED SPOON: We just use branches to fish things out of hot water or oil, but we want you to be safe!

WOODEN SPOON: For both mixing and cooking—you don't want to damage your cast iron, so always use wood, which won't scratch it.

FOREST HACK

When we're in the forest, we frequently use a combination spoon/fork/knife camp utensil for our measurements, so we tend to think in terms of "1 spoon of oregano" or "2 spoons of mustard." Because our viewers always ask about our ingredients, we've given more precise measurements here. For things like bread and pasta, stick with the measures we provide. For other things, like sauces and general seasonings, go ahead and use your spork—start small and taste as you go, adding more of what tastes good to you.

INGREDIENTS

We can't say it often enough: Food is an adventure! Look at these recipes like a map. You can follow them precisely, or you can veer off on your own and discover something entirely new. If you think you can add something to make a dish better, please do it! Similarly, if we call for a yellow onion, but all you have is red, use it. If there's an ingredient you don't like, use something you do like. Because meals take longer to prepare in the woods than they do in the kitchen, you'll find that everything just tastes *better*, regardless of whether you use the same ingredients we do (though, we do prefer salted butter because we didn't have it as children in Poland, and it's really quite amazing).

HEAT VS. FLAME

Even when you're cooking over your own grill at home, it's not always easy to control the heat—fire is unpredictable! But building a proper campfire with plenty of glowing embers takes time, at least 45 minutes. When you're out in the forest, among the elements, it proves even more difficult (just ask us about making bread in a light Irish rain). What starts out as a pleasant day could turn into a windy or drizzly evening come dinnertime. For us, the wind is the worst, but even your elevation can be a factor in how your food cooks. Where we live, we can experience the four seasons every 15 minutes, but this is what keeps it exciting.

First, know your woods—in both senses of the word. Are you allowed to gather downed branches where you are, or do you need to bring in your own firewood? Are you allowed to start a fire, and do you need a permit to do so? (The first time we made pierogi in the forest, some people reported us to the police! Luckily, we weren't breaking any laws, so they didn't fine us.) Depending on the type of wood you use, you could have a hotter fire or one that burns quickly; hardwood (trees with leaves) will burn longer than softwood (trees with needles). Avoid trees with needles anyway, as they also contain resin, which will produce a lot of smoke; and of course, older, drier wood burns better overall.

Keep in mind that our fire is not your fire. We do our best to indicate the amount of heat you should use, and our cooking is always over direct flame or coals. We most frequently use a medium fire, where the flames are just licking the bottom of the pan and you can hold your hand 4 inches (10 cm) above the pan for 4 to 5 seconds. With cast iron, that's the best heat to use so you don't burn your food. Though it takes a while to heat up and we do not preheat the pan, the iron does maintain the heat. The main thing to watch for when cooking over an open flame is not allowing that flames to engulf the pan.

Many of our recipes call for two types of heat—perhaps high heat first to bring water to a boil and then medium heat to cook the final dish. This means controlling the fire—whether that's building it up or letting it die down a bit. You can hasten the dying down by breaking up the central pile of coals or wood; if your firepit has the space, spread out the fire, so it's not so concentrated under your pan.

On a grill, you can easily set up two cooking zones by creating areas of direct heat and indirect heat. Bank the coals higher on one side, where the food will cook faster and get a better sear; food won't scorch on the "cooler" side, where the coals are lower (or even nonexistent). A gas grill is even easier to control for these zones. Either way, preheat the grill for a good 10 minutes before cooking. To get the most out of our recipes, we recommend using cast-iron cookware, whatever manner of flame you're cooking over; save your fancy cookware for the kitchen.

Even though they're similar methods of cooking, the amount of cook time between grill and campfire will likely differ. Remember: Our fire is not your fire, and these recipes are not

the same as "grilling," which applies flame and smoke directly to food. We provide a lot of visual markers to gauge when something is done, rather than telling you to cook for precisely so many minutes. That said, you have to pay attention every single minute. Did the wind just push the fire from the firepit, so there's nothing under your pan? Are you down to embers when you should have a bit more heat and flame? Pay attention to your fire and you will be rewarded.

Coals

You'll see that a lot of our recipes call for a putting a "handful" of coals on top of an inverted skillet. This is where that heavy-duty oven mitt comes in handy, but you can also use a small camp shovel or long tongs. We do this to create a sort of Dutch oven, though we keep the pan over a very low flame or smoldering coals rather than resting it directly in the coals. You'll need a fire that's been burning for at least 1 hour so you have enough embers to provide top heat while also maintaining heat from below. (On a grill, use the indirect-heat side and close the lid.)

For longer-cooking recipes, you might need to stoke the coals and replenish those on top. Resist the urge to peek at your food! Every time you take a look, the temperature inside your "camp oven" drops. We give a general timing to gauge when the dishes are done, but you can typically trust your nose—when you can smell it, it's nearly ready.

A NOTE ON CLEANING UP

We get a lot of questions about cleanliness, like, "How do we wash our hands after handling raw chicken?" We like to keep things clean and tidy; we just don't find this behind-the-scenes stuff all that filmable. We often find a cooking spot near a little stream, and yes, we do use a planet-friendly soap. Obviously, keep your food cold (40°F, or 4°C), and keep raw proteins separate from other raw foods to avoid contamination. Use separate cutting boards for veggies and proteins (or prep the veggies first). Have a bucket of water (or fire extinguisher) at the ready, and properly put out your fire before you leave. And, of course, carry out what you carry in—don't leave litter behind.

> ## FOREST HACK
> The cardinal rule of cooking with cast iron is taking proper care of it. The best way that we've found to clean our skillet is to put it over high heat and burn off everything. Then, we scrub it a little bit with a wooden utensil, sprinkle it with salt, and scrub some more. When you're done (and while it's still a little warm), rub the thinnest film of oil around the inside to season it.

BUSHCRAFT
How to Cook Like We Do

We cook outdoors more often than we cook at home—that's the truth. In the kitchen, dinner takes 1 hour, maybe 1½ hours, to prepare, but in the woods, with recording, it could take 6 hours or more. For that reason (and so many others), everything tastes much, much better when cooked outside. Above all, we want you to experience this—just go out there and make something delicious.

To help you cook like we do, we've included special "bushcraft" how-tos throughout the book, but it's important for us to note that no trees were harmed while bushcrafting for this book. Because we want to preserve our favorite place, all bushcrafting is done with felled trees and limbs from deciduous trees. To make a recipe the way we do, first read it thoroughly, so you know which type of setup to use; in some recipes, we use two different setups. For example, we might need to boil a pot of water and then cook chicken in a skillet, which would require two different bushcrafts (the pan stand and the pot stand). If you're using a grill or cooking over a grate at a campsite, it's not that big of a deal, but for us, we need to have our setups cut and ready to assemble when the time comes. We prepare both setups ahead, so it's easy to switch them in the middle of a recipe.

How to Light Your Fire

Lighting a fire does not have to be difficult. We don't even use matches! All you need is a knife and a flint. We can tell you that making fire in this way brings you back to basics and is really satisfying. You will understand as soon as you try it. Here's how:

1. The first thing you need to do is to find resin, which helps keep your fire alive. Choose a coniferous tree (such as a pine) and then look for an "injury" to the bark—usually where a limb has fallen or there's some other gash in the tree. It'll look white or yellowish and will have a strong evergreen scent.

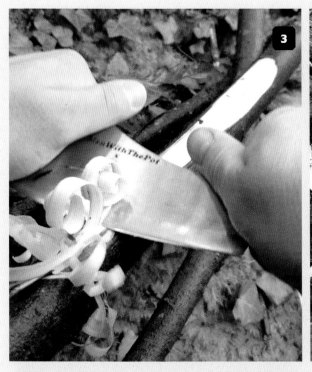

2. Use a small camp knife to flake a bit off the edges of the injured bark from the tree, scraping a little of the resin into your hand or other vessel. Take only the crystalized resin, and not anything that is oozing, as this protects the tree. (The dry stuff is also easier to handle.)

3. Find a few dry branches from a hardwood tree and use your knife to make some wood shavings. You'll need a handful.

4. Place the wood shavings and resin into the firepit (we often use a big tree stump that becomes a magnificent vessel for hot coals). Rub your knife against the flint to make a spark onto the shavings. Be patient, as it may take minute or two. It all depends on how dry your shavings are.

5. Continue to build your fire, adding smaller pieces of dry hardwood kindling (small sticks or twigs) and larger pieces of firewood. Let the fire burn for at least 30 minutes, but preferably 45, before you start cooking.

BUSHCRAFT
Make Your Own Pan Stand

This is by far our most-used bushcraft. You can make this remarkably simple pan stand from material you can find in *any* forest—simplicity is the beauty of it! We can assure you that going through all this hassle to place a pan over the fire will make your food taste a hundred times better, and we highly recommend doing this with kids or simply just to impress your significant other. (It works!) Here's how:

1. Find a fallen branch about 5 inches (13 cm) in diameter. Sharpen one end of the branch using a hatchet.

2. Stand the branch beside your fire and measure the approximate height where you'll want to place your pan. Remember you'll need enough space to build a fire and allow for airflow beneath the pan.

3. Use a handsaw to make a small groove that is the same thickness as your pan's handle. Don't go too deep with the groove, which could cause the branch to break while your food is cooking. (That has happened to us, and it's far from a pleasant experience!)

4. Use the blunt end of your hatchet to "hammer" the pointy end of the branch into the ground next to your fire.

5. Place your pan's handle in the groove and you are ready to go. (If it happens that your pan ends up being too loose, use a small piece of wood, like a shim, to keep it stable.)

BUSHCRAFT
Make Your Own Cooking Pot Stand

Obviously, if you're using a grill or campground firepit with cooking grates, that's going to be sturdy enough to hold a cast-iron pot filled with water; we sometimes use a pot stand. But when you're out in the forest, you might find yourself in need of a hands-free way to hold a pot over the flame. If you've watched enough of our videos, you know we use a couple different methods of holding the pot. Choose which method works best for you:

OPTION 1: Make a stronger version of the Noodle Drying Rack on page 28, using larger branches (about 2 inches, or 5 cm, in diameter) that are strong enough to support the pot and whatever's going in it.

OPTION 2: Tripod Potholder (see page 93).

OPTION 3: Follow the directions for Make Your Own Pan Stand (see page 20), cutting a strong limb, about the width of your palm and about 3 feet (90 cm) long. Use your hatchet to carve one end to a large point. This is your upright post.

1. Cut a branch, about 2 inches (5 cm) in diameter and a couple feet (60 cm) long.

2. Near the top of the upright post, use your handsaw to carve out a chunk from one side that's large enough for the smaller branch to be inserted into horizontally.

3. Use the head of your hatchet or a mallet to pound one end of the smaller branch into the notch of the upright post.

4. Pound the pointy end of the upright post into the ground next to the fire, so the smaller cross-limb hangs over the fire. It should be high enough so it won't burn, but low enough so the pot hanging by its handle is in the flames of a medium fire.

5. Test the strength of your setup, with water in the pot, before proceeding.

FOREST COOKING AROUND THE WORLD

As expats living in Northern Ireland, we're lucky that we get to spend our days in the beautiful forest, no matter the season—rain or shine. We apply this spirit of adventure to our cooking. Food should be fun! Use it to explore your world and broaden the choices of what you normally eat for dinner. In this chapter, we offer our own spin on recipes from such places as Poland (and its incredible street food called *zapiekanka*), Italy (with a meaty ragù and from-scratch tagliatelle), Spain (with a fresh take on paella), and beyond. As always, we encourage you to put your own take on the food.

CHICKEN ALFREDO WITH A TWIST

A typical Alfredo sauce consists of butter, cream, and Parmesan cheese. Our "twisted" version adds not only earthy mushrooms but also egg yolks for more body, and lemon zest for pop. We say, try it—it just might become your new favorite way to eat chicken.

INGREDIENTS

Table salt

For the pasta dough

1⅔ cups (200 g) all-purpose flour, plus more for dusting

2 large eggs

3 large egg yolks

1 tablespoon (15 ml) olive oil, plus 1 teaspoon (optional)

Pinch of table salt

For the chicken and sauce

2 chicken breasts

Flaky sea salt

Freshly cracked black pepper

2 tablespoons (30 ml) olive oil

½ cup plus 2 tablespoons (150 ml) white wine

1 yellow onion, very finely diced

2 tablespoons (30 g) butter

5⅓ ounces (150 g) white or brown mushrooms, thinly sliced

1 garlic clove, sliced

½ cup plus 2 tablespoons (150 ml) milk

½ cup (50 g) grated Parmesan, plus more for garnish

2 large egg yolks

1 tablespoon (6 g) grated lemon zest

Large handful of fresh parsley, coarsely chopped, plus more for garnish

1 teaspoon dried oregano

1 teaspoon table salt

1 teaspoon ground black pepper

DIRECTIONS

Prepare your fire for high heat. (If using a grill, set up one side for high heat and one side for medium heat.)

Fill a large pot with 2 quarts (about 2 L) water, generously season the water with table salt, and bring it to a boil over high heat.

To make the pasta dough

Mound the flour on a large cutting board and create a well in the middle. Crack the eggs into the well, add the yolks, drizzle in the oil (if using), and sprinkle with table salt. Using a fork, break up the eggs and gradually start stirring in flour from the mound until all the flour is fully incorporated and you have a dry, craggy-looking dough ball (you might have to use your hands near the end). Knead until a smooth, stiff, yet pliable dough ball forms, 8 to 10 minutes.

continued

BUSHCRAFT
Make Your Own Noodle Drying Rack

There are as many ways to make fresh pasta as there are types of pasta. Some of our recipes call for resting; some call for tossing right into the boiling water; and some call for drying, which helps the noodles retain their shape when boiled. Here's how to create a forest-made drying rack:

1. Choose two branches of about equal size, about 1 inch (2.5 cm) in diameter, with a forked branch on one end.

2. For each, cut down the forked branches to 2 or 3 inches (5 or 7.5 cm), and whittle the opposite end to a point.

3. Stick the pointed end of the branches into the ground a couple feet (60 cm) apart.

4. Find a relatively straight stick that can rest between the two forks and whittle it clean of bark before setting it between the forks.

Generously dust the board and dough with flour. Use a rolling pin to roll the dough very thin, about $\frac{1}{16}$ inch (0.16 cm) thick, and about the size of your board (ours is 11 × 18 inches, or 28 × 45 cm). Cut the dough into strips, about $\frac{1}{4}$ inch (0.6 cm) wide (see Forest Hack, below). Sprinkle with flour and gently toss to loosen the noodles. Hang them over a drying rack (see Bushcraft, page 28) or the back of a clean chair to dry while you prep the remaining ingredients and the water comes to boil. (Touching is okay, but try not to overlap or clump the noodles.)

Add the noodles to the boiling water. Stir to separate them and boil just until cooked through, about 90 seconds. Drain, reserving a bit of the cooking water. Place the noodles in a bowl with a bit of cool water mixed with a bit of the cooking water, just enough to coat but not submerge the noodles.

To make the chicken and sauce
Prepare your fire for medium heat.

Generously sprinkle the chicken on both sides with sea salt and cracked pepper.

Pour the oil into a large cast-iron skillet over medium heat and heat until it shimmers. Add the chicken and

cook until deep golden brown on both sides and cooked through (when the juices run clear). Add the wine and cook until slightly reduced. Transfer the chicken to a cutting board to rest.

Add the onion to the skillet. Cook, stirring frequently, until the wine has evaporated and the onion is very tender and browned. Add the butter to melt, then add the mushrooms and cook until softened and brown. Add the garlic and cook for 1 minute more. Pour in the milk, stirring well.

In a small bowl, stir together the Parm, egg yolks, and lemon zest. Spoon the mixture into the mushroom sauce, stirring well to combine. Stir in a handful of parsley and the oregano, table salt, and ground pepper.

Slice the chicken and return it to the skillet, stirring to coat with the sauce and heat through. Add the noodles to the skillet and toss to coat with the sauce. Taste for seasoning. Sprinkle with more Parm and parsley before serving.

FOREST HACK

Here's an easy way to cut noodles evenly: Pick up either the top or bottom edge of the well-floured dough and fold it on itself, accordion style, folding back and forth four times, for a total of five layers. It will look like a neatly folded letter, the width of your board. To form the noodles, simply cut across the pleats every $\frac{1}{4}$ inch (0.6 cm) or so.

GNOCCHI, TWO WAYS

If you've ever ordered gnocchi at a restaurant and been surprised at the price, you'll be even more surprised to learn how easy it is to make—even in the forest. If you can't find Yukon gold potatoes (or Maris Piper in Europe), russets work just fine.

INGREDIENTS

For the gnocchi dough

About 1 pound, 2 ounces (500 g) Yukon gold or Maris Piper potatoes

1 large egg

2 teaspoons table salt

1 teaspoon ground black pepper

Scant 1½ cups (175 g) all-purpose flour, plus more for dusting

For the sauces

3 tablespoons (45 g) butter, divided

1 shallot, finely chopped

6 garlic cloves, 3 left whole, 3 sliced, divided

Chopped fresh parsley for garnish

3 tomatoes, finely diced

¾ cup plus 1 tablespoon plus 1 teaspoon (200 ml) vegetable stock

3 tablespoons plus ½ teaspoon (50 g) tomato paste

1 teaspoon red pepper flakes

1 teaspoon dried oregano

1 teaspoon table salt

1 teaspoon ground black pepper

Grated Parmesan cheese for garnish

DIRECTIONS

Prepare your fire for high heat. (If using a grill, set up one side for high heat and one side for medium heat.)

To make the dough

Fill a large pot with 2 quarts (about 2 L) water and bring it to a boil over high heat. Add the potatoes and boil until tender and easily pierced with a skewer, 20 to 30 minutes. Meanwhile, prep the remaining ingredients.

When the potatoes are done, remove them from the water and cool just enough so you can peel them. (Return the water to the flame and bring it back to a boil.) Place the peeled potatoes in a large bowl and mash. Add the egg, salt, and pepper and mash until creamy. Sprinkle the flour over the top and knead it into the potatoes until you have a sticky dough ball.

Dust a cutting board with flour and place the dough on it. Knead until a soft dough forms and the flour is fully incorporated—but do not overwork it; the dough should still feel soft. Cut off a chunk of dough (about the size of your palm). Gently roll it under your hands to make a rope, about the length of your board and about the thickness of your index finger. Now, cut the rope into 1-inch (2.5 cm) pieces.

Lightly flour the gnocchi board (see Bushcraft, page 32). Roll each 1-inch (2.5 cm) piece of dough down along the ridges of the gnocchi board, pressing with your thumb. You only have to roll each piece over itself once or twice, or a couple inches (5 cm) from the edge of the board.

Add the gnocchi to the boiling water and boil until they float, 2 to 3 minutes. Remove from the water (see Forest Hack, page 32) and continue with the rest of the dough. (If one or two "ropes" is all you need for now, wrap up the dough and keep it cold for up to 1 day. If you're at home, make all the gnocchi, set on a baking sheet so they don't touch each other, freeze until solid, then transfer to a freezer-safe container or bag for longer storage.)

Prepare your fire for medium heat.

continued

FOREST HACK

To keep the gnocchi from sticking together while you make the sauces, place them in a bowl with some of the cooking water and a bit of cold water mixed in—just enough to dampen the gnocchi, not submerge them.

To make the sauces

In a large cast-iron skillet over medium heat, melt 2 tablespoons (30 g) butter. Add about one-quarter of the shallot and the 3 whole garlic cloves and cook until sizzling and softened. Add half the gnocchi to the skillet and cook for a couple minutes, stirring, until golden. Sprinkle with parsley and remove from the heat. Transfer the gnocchi to a serving dish and clean the skillet.

Return the clean skillet to medium heat and add the remaining 1 tablespoon (15 g) of butter to melt. Add the remaining shallot and the sliced garlic and cook until sizzling and softened. Add the tomatoes and stir to heat through, then stir in the stock. Bring to a good bubble, then stir in the tomato paste, red pepper flakes, oregano, salt, and black pepper. Cook for a couple minutes until reduced, creating a thick, bubbly sauce. Add the remaining gnocchi and stir to coat. Remove from the heat.

Serve both gnocchi alongside one another. Sprinkle generously with Parmesan and more parsley to serve.

BUSHCRAFT
Make Your Own Gnocchi Board

Gnocchi gets its signature ridged look from being rolled across a specialized wooden plank called a gnocchi board. You *can* use the tines of a fork, or you can create your own board. Here's how:

1. Choose a downed limb about the width of your fist and cut it about the length of two palms.

2. Split the piece down the middle vertically. Choose one half and toss the other half on the fire.

3. With the tip of a sharp blade, create 5 or 6 channels down the inner (cut) side of the wood. (They don't have to be very deep, and you don't have to carve channels across the whole piece; 5 or 6 will do.) Blow off any shavings.

4. Hang the channel side above the flames for a minute or so to seal the cut edge.

POLISH ROLADY

Brace yourself for total meat madness. Rolady (think: roulades or roll-ups) was a popular dish served to Polish nobility. It's a cut of meat that's rolled around a variety of fillings and then seared and braised until tender. You will definitely earn your crown when you make these in the forest.

INGREDIENTS

About 11 ounces (300 g) smoked pork belly

5⅓ ounces (150 g; 2 links) Polish sausage (smoked kielbasa)

2 Polish dill pickles, finely diced

2 (7-ounce, or 200 g) pieces thin-cut top round steak

4 tablespoons (60 g) Dijon or spicy brown mustard

Flaky sea salt

Freshly cracked black pepper

1 large yellow onion, thinly sliced

1 to 2 tablespoons (15 to 30 ml) olive oil

3 garlic cloves, chopped

1¼ cups (300 ml) beef or chicken stock

1 teaspoon dried marjoram

1 teaspoon table salt

1 teaspoon ground black pepper

3 bay leaves

1¼ cups (300 ml) water, divided

2 tablespoons (15 g) all-purpose flour

Chopped fresh chives for garnish

DIRECTIONS

Prepare your fire for medium heat.

Slice four pieces, about ¼ inch (0.6 cm) thick, from the pork belly and set aside. Dice the remaining pork belly.

Halve one sausage link crosswise, then halve it lengthwise and set aside. Dice the remaining sausage.

Cut the pickles lengthwise into four slices of even thickness. Set aside four of the center "planks" and finely dice the remaining pickles.

Set one piece of beef on a cutting board and pound it to ¼ inch (0.6 cm) thick. Spread 2 tablespoons (30 g) mustard across the beef and sprinkle with sea salt and cracked pepper. In the center of the beef, place two pieces of pork belly, two pieces of sausage, two pickle slices, and a small handful of onion. Starting with a long side, fold the beef over the filings and roll it up. Thread a wooden skewer through the flap to secure the beef. (To make your own skewers, see page 68, or make them similar to how you make chopsticks, page 46.) Repeat with the remaining beef and sliced ingredients.

continued

BUSHCRAFT
Make Your Own Meat Mallet

Top round is a little less tender than other cuts of meat, but pounding it helps tenderize the meat. You can use a meat tenderizer, or you can make your own mallet. Here's how:

1. Find a downed tree limb about the diameter that you can wrap your hand around and just about touch your middle finger to your thumb.

2. To make the mallet head, saw off a piece of the limb about two hand-widths long. Whittle 1 to 2 inches (2.5 to 5 cm) of bark off each end.

3. To make the handle, cut a thinner branch, 1 to 2 inches (2.5 to 5 cm) in diameter, 12 to 18 inches (30 to 45 cm) long. Whittle one end of the handle to make a little bit of a point.

4. Use the tip of a knife to dig out a hole from the middle of the mallet head, where the pointed end of the handle will go.

5. Tap the handle into the hole. Hold the mallet head over a flame to seal the cut edges.

Heat a large cast-iron skillet over medium heat and pour in the oil. When smoking, set the rolady into the skillet, skewer-side down. Cook until a nice brown sear forms on the bottom, then turn and repeat searing until all sides have a good sear on them. Transfer to a cutting board to rest.

In the skillet, place the remaining sliced onion and cook until golden and softened. Add the garlic and cook for 1 minute more. Add the diced pork belly and diced sausage and cook until browned and the fat is rendered. Stir in the diced pickles, stock, spices, and bay leaves and bring to a boil. Add the rolady to the skillet and bring the broth to a

full boil. Cover with an inverted skillet (or close the grill lid) and cook for 45 minutes. Turn the rolady, add 1 cup (240 ml) water (or enough to just about cover the meat), and re-cover. Finish cooking for another 15 to 20 minutes.

In a small bowl, stir together the flour and remaining ¼ cup (60 ml) of water until smooth. Transfer the rolady to a cutting board. Stir the flour slurry into the broth and simmer until thickened. Remove the skillet from the heat.

Remove the skewers from the rolady and slice as desired. Spoon the sauce over the slices and sprinkle with chives.

PAELLA WITH CHORIZO

This recipe caused a lot of angst among our viewers! They hated that we added chorizo (which, traditionally, is not part of paella). But we love the added crunchiness once it's cooked and crisp. Because we feel you're supposed to have fun and explore with your food, we say try it! If you don't like it, leave it out next time. The best paella rice is a short-grain rice, such as bomba. If you can't find it, arborio makes a surprisingly good substitute, as does Calrose.

INGREDIENTS

$1\frac{2}{3}$ cups (400 ml) chicken stock

Large pinch of saffron threads

$5\frac{1}{3}$ ounces (150 g) smoked chorizo, very thinly sliced

2 chicken breasts, cut into 1-inch (2.5 cm) pieces

2 tablespoons (30 ml) olive oil

1 yellow onion, diced

3 garlic cloves, sliced

1 red bell pepper, diced

1 teaspoon smoked paprika

$12\frac{1}{2}$ ounces (350 g) paella rice

2 tomatoes, diced

$\frac{1}{3}$ cup (50 g) fresh peas, or scant $\frac{1}{2}$ cup (50 g) frozen and thawed

6 medium or large shrimp, peeled and deveined

1 lemon, cut into wedges

Chopped fresh parsley for garnish

DIRECTIONS

Prepare your fire for medium heat.

Pour the stock into your camp cup and place it near the campfire (or pour it into a small saucepan and place it on the grill). Add the saffron threads.

In a large cast-iron skillet over medium heat, cook the chorizo until golden and curled on both sides. Remove the chorizo from the skillet and add the chicken to the fat that remained behind. Cook until browned on all sides (it doesn't have to be cooked through at this point). Remove from the skillet.

Pour the oil into the skillet and heat until hot. Add the onion and garlic and cook, stirring frequently, until browned and the vegetables start to soften. Stir in the bell pepper and cook for 2 minutes more. Stir in the paprika until everything is well coated. Add the rice and cook, stirring, until lightly toasted, about 1 minute. Add the warmed stock and bring the mixture to a boil.

Add the chicken and tomatoes. Stir to evenly distribute the ingredients, cover with an inverted skillet (or close the grill lid), and cook until the rice is tender and most of the stock is absorbed, 15 to 20 minutes.

Stir in the chorizo and peas, taking care not to disturb the rice on the bottom of the skillet. Dot the top with the shrimp, re-cover the skillet, and cook until the stock is fully absorbed and the shrimp is cooked through, just a few minutes. Remove from the heat.

Garnish with a squeeze of lemon juice and parsley before digging in.

PIEROGI FROM SCRATCH

In Poland, pierogi are a traditional dish served on Christmas Eve—but we don't think you should wait until December to make them. We're calling for cottage cheese here, which is the English translation for the Polish word *twaróg*, a dry cow's milk cheese. The cottage cheese you might be used to, however, is very creamy and wet; if you use that in pierogi, the dough won't stick together and you'll have a mess. The cheese we use has no moisture, more of a skimmed version of cottage cheese. A good substitute would be farmer's cheese or quark.

DIRECTIONS

Prepare your fire for high heat. (If using a grill, set up one side for high heat and one side for medium heat.)

To start the filling
Fill a large pot with 2 quarts (about 2 L) water, generously season the water with salt, and bring it to a boil over high heat. Add the potatoes and boil until tender and easily pierced with a skewer, about 20 minutes. Remove the potatoes from the water and set aside. Reserve the hot water for later. Meanwhile, prep the dough and the filling.

To make the dough
Mound the flour on a large cutting board and create a well in the middle. Pour about half the warm water into the well along with the oil and kosher salt. Gradually stir the flour from the mound into the water, adding more water as it gets dry, until all the flour is incorporated and you have a dry, craggy-looking dough ball (you might have to use your hands near the end). Knead until a smooth dough ball forms, 6 to 8 minutes. Set the dough aside while you finish the filling.

Prepare your fire for medium heat.

To finish the filling
Cut two strips, about ⅓-inch (0.85 cm) thick, off the pork belly and set aside. Dice the remaining pork belly and place it in a large cast-iron skillet over medium heat. Cook until the fat is rendered and the pork is golden. Scoot the pieces to one side of the skillet and add the pork strips. Cook until golden, brown, and delicious on both sides, a few minutes more.

Remove the pork and all but a film of fat from the skillet and add the onion to the skillet. Cook until deeply golden and very soft.

Meanwhile, transfer the potatoes to a large bowl and mash until somewhat creamy. Add the cottage cheese, cooked onions, pork pieces (reserving a small bit for garnish), table salt, and pepper and mix well.

continued

INGREDIENTS

For the filling

2 large Yukon gold or Maris Piper potatoes, peeled and halved

7 ounces (200 g) smoked pork belly

1 yellow onion, diced

5⅓ ounces (150 g) cottage cheese (see headnote)

2 teaspoons table salt

1 teaspoon ground black pepper

For the dough

2½ cups (300 g) all-purpose flour, plus more for dusting

¾ cup plus 1 tablespoon plus 1 teaspoon (200 ml) warm water

1 tablespoon plus 1 teaspoon (20 ml) olive oil

1 teaspoon kosher salt

For finishing and serving

2 tablespoons (30 g) butter

2 tablespoons (30 g) sour cream

Chopped fresh chives for garnish

Return the reserved pot of water to the heat and bring it to a low boil.

Dust a cutting board with flour. Halve the dough and set aside one half. Give the other half a few kneads, then roll it out on the prepared board until about 1/16 inch (0.16 cm) thick, or about the size of your board (ours is 11 × 18 inches, or 28 × 45 cm). Use your camp cup to cut circles from the dough (you'll get five or six rounds). Repeat with the other half of the dough.

Spoon a heaping tablespoon of filling into the center of each piece of dough, fold the dough over the filling, and pinch the edges shut, forming a half-moon shape. (Form the filling into a quenelle, or oval shape, rather than a round golf-ball shape [see page 71 on how to make quenelles], to better fill the dough.) Once all the pierogi are made, use a fork to press and seal the edges.

Add the pierogi to the boiling water and cook until they float. Remove from the heat.

To finish and serve the pierogi
Return the skillet to the heat and add the butter to melt. Add half the pierogi and cook until golden on both sides. Serve alongside the unfried pierogi. (Alternatively, fry them all—or not—do what you like best!) Dollop with sour cream and sprinkle with the reserved pork belly pieces and chopped chives. Serve with the fried pork belly strips.

CAMPFIRE RAVIOLI

Homemade (or, in our case, forest-made) pasta is really so much better than anything you buy. Our dough recipe even works for filled pastas such as ravioli. When you try this earthy mushroom filling, combined with the creamy sauce, you'll never want to have pasta any other way.

DIRECTIONS

Prepare your fire for medium heat. (If using a grill, set up one side for high heat and one side for medium heat.)

To make the dough

Mound the flour on a large cutting board and create a well in the middle. Crack the eggs into the well, pour in the oil (if using), and add the salt. Using a fork, break up the eggs and gradually stir in flour from the mound until all the flour is fully incorporated and you have a dry, craggy-looking dough ball (you might have to use your hands near the end). Knead until a smooth, stiff, yet pliable dough ball forms, 8 to 10 minutes. Set aside, covered with a bowl, while you prep the filling.

To make the filling

In a large cast-iron skillet over medium heat, heat the olive oil until hot. Toss in the shallots, reserving a small handful for later, and cook just until they start to turn color. Add the mushrooms, garlic, thyme, a big pinch of salt, and a few grinds of cracked pepper. Cook, stirring occasionally, until the vegetables are softened and brown. Add a big pinch of Parm and give it all a good stir. Mix in the ricotta and the parsley and remove the skillet from the heat.

To make the sauce

Place a second clean skillet over medium heat and pour in the oil. When hot, add the reserved handful of shallot and cook, stirring, just until it starts to turn color. Stir in the cream and bring it to a boil. Add the remaining Parmesan (from the filling), salt, and ground pepper and stir until melted, well combined, and thickened. Sprinkle in the parsley, remove from the heat, and cover to keep warm.

Prepare your fire for high heat.

Fill a large pot with 2 quarts (about 2 L) water, generously season the water with salt, and bring it to a boil over high heat.

continued

INGREDIENTS

For the pasta dough

2 heaping cups (250 g) all-purpose flour, plus more for dusting

3 large eggs

1 tablespoon plus 1 teaspoon (20 ml) olive oil (optional)

1 teaspoon table salt

For the filling

1 to 2 tablespoons (15 to 30 ml) olive oil

2 shallots, finely chopped

1½ cups (150 g) mushrooms, very thinly sliced

3 garlic cloves, thinly sliced

1 thyme sprig, leaves stripped

Table salt

Freshly cracked black pepper

1¾ ounces (50 g) Parmesan cheese, grated

½ cup plus scant 2 tablespoons (150 g) ricotta

Small handful of fresh parsley leaves, torn

For the sauce

1 tablespoon (15 ml) olive oil

½ cup plus 2 tablespoons (150 ml) heavy cream

½ teaspoon table salt

½ teaspoon ground black pepper

Small handful of fresh parsley leaves, chopped, plus more for garnish

To make the ravioli
Generously flour the cutting board and place the dough on it. Use a rolling pin to roll the dough to about ⅛ inch (0.3 cm) thick, or about the height of your board, 12 inches (30 cm) or so. Trim the edges to create a rectangle. Halve the dough horizontally.

Dollop the mushroom filling in four or five even spoonfuls lengthwise down the middle of one sheet of dough. Fold the bottom portion of dough over the filling so the edges meet at the top. Using your fingers, gently press around the mounds to lightly seal the dough. Run your knife along the top edge to make the edges even, then cut between the ravioli, leaving about a ½-inch (1 cm) border around each mound. Use the tines of a fork to firmly press and seal the edges of the ravioli. Repeat with the other sheet of dough and the remaining filling.

Add the ravioli to the boiling water and cook until tender—it'll be a couple minutes, just until they float; don't overcook them. Transfer the ravioli from the water to a bowl or plate.

Spoon the sauce over the ravioli, garnishing with more chopped parsley.

FOREST TAKEAWAY

Whether you call it "takeout" or "takeaway," you won't get a dish this good anywhere else. In fact, when we developed this recipe, we really couldn't get it anywhere else! All the takeout places were closed due to the coronavirus pandemic, and we were thinking about all the delicious food we couldn't order—so, we decided to make it ourselves. Be sure to use bread flour for these noodles, as they need the extra strength it provides.

INGREDIENTS

For the noodles
2½ cups (300 g) bread flour, plus more for dusting

½ cup plus 2 tablespoons (150 ml) warm water (see Forest Hack)

1 teaspoon table salt

For the chicken and sauce
2 chicken breasts, cut into 1-inch (2.5 cm) pieces

½ teaspoon table salt

½ teaspoon ground black pepper

1 generous glug soy sauce, plus scant ¼ cup (50 ml)

1 tablespoon (9.5 g) potato starch or (8 g) cornstarch

Oil for frying

½ to 1 teaspoon sesame seeds

1 spring onion, sliced

3 garlic cloves, sliced

1 carrot, julienned

1- to 2-inch (2.5 to 5 cm) piece fresh ginger, peeled and julienned

2½ tablespoons (50 g) honey

2 tablespoons (30 ml) rice vinegar

1 tablespoon (15 g) brown sugar

1 tablespoon (16 g) tomato paste

Chopped fresh parsley for garnish

DIRECTIONS

Prepare your fire for high heat. (If using a grill, set up one side for high heat and one side for medium heat.)

Fill a large pot with 2 quarts (about 2 L) water and bring it to a gentle boil over high heat.

To make the noodles
Mound the flour on a large cutting board and create a well in the middle. Pour about half the warm water into the well and sprinkle with the salt. Gradually stir the flour from the mound into the water, adding more water as it gets dry, until all the flour is fully incorporated and you have a dry, craggy-looking dough ball (you might have to use your hands near the end). Knead until a smooth dough ball forms, 8 to 10 minutes.

Generously dust a cutting board with flour and place the dough on it. Roll the dough very thin, about the height of your board, or 12 × 12 inches (30 × 30 cm). Cut strips of dough, about ¼ inch (0.6 cm) wide (see Forest Hack, page 46). Sprinkle the strips with flour and gently toss to loosen the noodles.

Add the noodles to the boiling water. Stir to separate them and boil just until cooked, about 90 seconds. Drain, reserving a bit of the cooking water. Place the noodles in a bowl with a bit of cool water mixed with a bit of the cooking water, just enough to coat but not submerge the noodles.

Prepare your fire for medium heat.

FOREST HACK

Put your water in a camp cup and set it next to your fire while you gather your ingredients. It'll be warm enough once you're ready to make your dough.

continued

BUSHCRAFT
Make Your Own Chopsticks

One reason we wanted to make this recipe was so we could use our forest-made chopsticks, which is basically Whittling 101. (They come in handy if you find yourself out in the forest without any utensils!) Here's how:

1. Choose two dry straight sticks about the same length and width that are comfortable enough to hold in your fingers, anywhere from 9 to 12 inches (23 to 30 cm) long and somewhere between ¼ and ½ inch (0.6 and 1 cm) in diameter.

2. With your sharp knife, working away from you, shave strips of wood from one end of each stick. Clean up a couple inches (about 5 cm) and whittle it down to about ¼ (0.6 cm) inch thick.

3. You can smooth the cut ends further by shaving smaller pieces, or you can hold the whittled ends briefly over the flame to seal the edges and remove any errant splinters.

FOREST HACK

Here's an easy way to cut noodles evenly: Pick up either the top or bottom edge of the well-floured dough and fold it on itself, accordion style, folding back and forth four times, for a total of five layers. It will look like a neatly folded letter, the width of your board. To form the noodles, simply cut across the pleats every ¼ inch (0.6 cm) or so.

To make the chicken and sauce

Put the chicken in a large bowl and sprinkle with the salt and pepper. Drizzle with a generous glug of soy sauce and toss to coat. Add the starch and mix well to coat.

Coat the bottom of a large cast-iron skillet with a solid layer of oil, about ⅛ inch (0.3 cm) deep, and place it over medium heat. When shimmering, add the chicken and cook until deep golden on all sides (it doesn't have to be fully cooked through at this point). Sprinkle with the sesame seeds and cook for 1 minute. Remove from the heat and transfer the chicken to a bowl.

Carefully wipe out the skillet, return it to the heat, and pour in 1 tablespoon (15 ml) oil. When hot, add the spring onion and garlic and cook until fragrant. Add the carrot and ginger and cook for a couple minutes more. Remove from the heat and transfer the vegetables to a bowl.

Carefully wipe out the skillet and return it to the heat. Pour in the remaining scant ¼ cup (50 ml) of soy sauce and add the honey, vinegar, brown sugar, tomato paste, and a splash of water. Stir to combine and bring the sauce to a rapid boil. Let the sauce cook and reduce in volume until it is quite thick and saucy.

Return the chicken to the skillet, stirring to coat with the sauce. Stir in the vegetable mixture. Continue to cook until the sauce is clinging to the chicken and vegetables, without much pooling in the skillet. Add the noodles and stir well to coat. Serve sprinkled with chopped parsley.

FOREST-MADE LASAGNA

Who says you can't make lasagna in the forest? The first time we tried this, it didn't really work out. The bottom burnt a bit, and so it became a personal challenge for us to do it properly. After some practice, now, we can honestly say this is better than you'd get in a restaurant.

INGREDIENTS

For the dough

Heaping 2 cups (250 g) all-purpose flour, plus more for dusting

3 large eggs

1 tablespoon (15 ml) olive oil (optional)

1 teaspoon table salt

For the filling

1 to 2 tablespoons (15 to 30 ml) olive oil

1 small yellow onion, finely chopped

4 garlic cloves, thinly sliced

About 11 ounces (300 g) ground beef

$\frac{1}{2}$ cup plus 2 tablespoons (150 ml) port

$\frac{3}{4}$ cup plus 1 heaping tablespoon (200 g) tomato sauce

1 teaspoon dried oregano

Table salt

Ground black pepper

Handful of small fresh basil leaves, plus more, chopped, for garnish

For the white sauce

$\frac{1}{2}$ cup plus 2 tablespoons (150 ml) milk

1 tablespoon plus 1 teaspoon (20 g) butter

1$\frac{1}{2}$ tablespoons (12 g) all-purpose flour

1 tablespoon (15 g) Dijon mustard

Table salt

Ground black pepper

Heaping $\frac{1}{3}$ cup (55 g) grated mozzarella cheese

For assembly

Olive oil

$\frac{2}{3}$ cup (100 g) cherry tomatoes, thinly sliced

1 cup (150 g) grated mozzarella cheese

DIRECTIONS

To make the dough

Prepare your fire for medium heat.

Mound the flour on a large cutting board and create a well in the middle. Crack the eggs into the well, pour in the oil (if using), and add the salt. Using a fork, break up the eggs and gradually start stirring in the flour from the mound until all the flour is fully incorporated and you have a dry, craggy-looking dough ball (you might have to use your hands near the end). Knead until a smooth, stiff, yet pliable, dough ball forms, 8 to 10 minutes.

Generously flour a clean board, place the dough on it, and generously sprinkle the dough with more flour. Divide the dough into three equal pieces and roll each piece until very thin (so you can almost see your fingers through it) and about the size of your skillet. Set aside.

To make the filling

Pour the oil into a large cast-iron skillet and place it over medium heat. When smoking, add the onion and garlic and cook until softened. Add the ground beef and cook until no longer pink. Carefully add the port—it will likely ignite; let it go!— and cook until reduced and the pan is nearly dry. (If you're using a gas grill, or this otherwise worries you, remove the skillet from the flame before adding the port, then return it to the heat.) Stir in the tomato sauce, oregano, 1 teaspoon salt, and 1 teaspoon pepper, mixing well. Taste for seasoning, toss in the basil leaves, and remove from the heat.

continued

To make the sauce

Pour the milk into a heatproof camp cup and set it near the coals (or set a small saucepan on the grill) and add the butter. When the butter melts, stir in the flour until combined (a few small clumps are okay). Stir in the mustard, 1 teaspoon salt, and 1 teaspoon pepper. Stir in the mozzarella until you have a smooth creamy sauce. Taste for seasoning and remove from the heat.

To assemble

Off heat, coat a clean cast-iron skillet with a film of oil. Place a large spoonful of filling in the skillet and spread it around (it won't cover the entire bottom of the skillet).

Lay one sheet of dough over the filling, and drizzle on one-third of the white sauce, allowing it to spread (it doesn't have to fully cover the dough). Spread a heaping spoonful of the filling over the sauce, sprinkle with half of the sliced tomatoes, and one-third of the mozzarella. Repeat with a similar layer.

For the final layer, set the last sheet of dough on top and drizzle with the remaining white sauce. Top with the remaining filling and remaining mozzarella.

Set the skillet over medium heat and invert another skillet over the top (or close the grill lid). Place a handful of coals on top and cook until the pasta is cooked through and the cheese is melted and golden, 25 to 30 minutes, replenishing the coals as needed. Sprinkle with chopped fresh basil before serving.

POLISH ZAPIEKANKA

Zapiekanka. You can't call this by any other name. It's Polish street food at its finest—and a great hangover meal! We call for red cheddar cheese, which is an aged English cheese called Red Leicester. If you can't find it, choose any aged cheddar.

DIRECTIONS

Prepare your fire for low or indirect heat.

To make the dough
In a large bowl, stir together the flour and yeast. Stir in the warm water, just until the flour is moistened (it won't all be combined). Create a well in the middle and add the milk, butter, and rosemary salt. Combine the mixture, then knead until a smooth dough ball forms, 8 to 10 minutes. Return the dough to the bowl, cover with another bowl, and set in a warm place (such as near the campfire) to let the dough rise. Meanwhile, prep the filling ingredients.

Set a well-seasoned cast-iron skillet over low heat/indirect heat.

continued

INGREDIENTS

For the bread dough

2 heaping cups (250 g) all-purpose flour, plus more for dusting

Scant 2 teaspoons active dry or instant yeast

1 cup plus 2 teaspoons (250 ml) warm water

½ cup plus 2 tablespoons (150 ml) milk

2 tablespoons plus 2 teaspoons (40 g) butter, at room temperature

1 teaspoon rosemary salt or table salt (see Make Your Own Rosemary Salt, on page 53)

Melted butter for drizzling

For the toppings

1 tablespoon (15 ml) oil

1 yellow onion, finely diced

2½ cups (250 g) white or brown mushrooms, thinly sliced

3 fresh chiles (red and green), finely chopped (seeds retained for more heat)

1 tablespoon (15 g) whole-grain mustard

1 teaspoon rosemary salt or table salt

1 teaspoon lemon pepper

3½ ounces (100 g) red cheddar cheese, grated

1 (7-ounce, or 200 g) block mozzarella cheese, cut lengthwise into 8 or 9 "sticks"

Chopped fresh chives for garnish

Dust a cutting board with flour and place the dough on it. Form the dough into a log the length of the bottom of your skillet. Place the dough in the skillet, drizzle it liberally with melted butter, and brush the dough to fully coat. Cover with an inverted skillet and top with a large handful of coals (or close the grill lid). Cook until the bread is golden and cooked through, 30 to 35 minutes, replenishing the coals as needed. Transfer the bread to a cutting board.

To make the filling
Pour the oil into a large cast-iron skillet and place it over low heat. When hot, add the onion and cook until softened. Add the mushrooms and cook until lightly browned. Add the chiles and cook until softened. Stir in the mustard, rosemary salt, and lemon pepper.

To assemble and serve
Halve the bread lengthwise, creating a top half and bottom half. Divide the filling between the halves. Set the halves, side by side, in a clean cast-iron skillet over very low or indirect heat. Sprinkle evenly with the cheddar. Lay the mozzarella sticks diagonally over both halves of bread in a crisscross pattern (as if the bread were one large piece). Cover with an inverted skillet and top with coals (or close the lid). Cook until the cheeses are melted and browned, 5 to 10 minutes. Transfer the entire melty loaf as one unit to the cutting board. Sprinkle with chives, then cut crosswise three times, making six pieces.

MAKE YOUR OWN ROSEMARY SALT

While you can find rosemary salt in the supermarket, it's very easy to make at home with a food processor. Pulse ¼ cup packed fresh rosemary leaves with ¼ cup coarse sea salt about 10 times, until the consistency of damp sand. Transfer to a bowl and stir in ¾ cup kosher salt. Mix well. Spread on a baking sheet to dry for a couple hours before transferring to an 8-ounce (240 ml) jar for storage.

TAGLIATELLE RAGÙ

A while back, we were talking to an Italian friend who mentioned ragù, a meaty tomato sauce, and we decided to go for it. We first learned how to make pasta watching online videos. Then, when we posted our own video, it got 20 million views in a few days—generating a lot of discussion! Initially, we put oil in the cooking water because we had been told long ago that's what you do to keep the pasta from sticking. People started arguing with each other in the comments: some said to do it, whereas others said there's no advantage to adding it. What we found is that when used in cast-iron cooking, the oil colors the water—and the pasta—so we started adding it to the dough instead. But we encourage you to do it your way.

INGREDIENTS

For the pasta dough

Table salt

1⅔ cups (200 g) all-purpose flour, plus more for dusting

2 large eggs

3 large egg yolks

1 tablespoon plus 1 teaspoon (20 ml) olive oil (optional)

For the ragù

1 tablespoon (15 ml) olive oil

1 large leek, white and light green parts, thoroughly rinsed, finely chopped

1 yellow onion, finely diced

1 large carrot, very finely diced

About 11 ounces (300 g) ground beef

1¼ cups (300 g) tomato sauce

¾ cup plus 1 tablespoon plus 1 teaspoon (200 ml) red wine

1 tablespoon (3 g) dried oregano

1 teaspoon table salt

1 teaspoon ground black pepper

½ cup (50 g) grated Parmesan cheese

Fresh basil for garnish

DIRECTIONS

Prepare your fire for high heat. (If using a grill, set up one side for high heat and one side for medium heat.)

To make the pasta

Fill a large pot with 2 quarts (about 2 L) water, generously season the water with salt, and bring it to a boil over high heat.

Mound the flour on a large cutting board and create a well in the middle. Crack the eggs into the well and add the egg yolks, oil (if using), and a large pinch of salt. Using a fork, break up the eggs and gradually stir in the flour from the mound until all the flour is fully incorporated and you have a dry, craggy-looking dough ball (you might have to use your hands near the end). Knead until a smooth, stiff, yet pliable dough ball forms, 8 to 10 minutes.

Generously flour the board and place the dough on it. Use a rolling pin to roll the dough to less than 1/16 inch (0.16 cm) thick, about 11 × 11 inches (28 × 28 cm). Cut strips of dough, between ¼ and ½ inch (0.6 and 1 cm) wide (see Forest Hack, page 56). Sprinkle with flour and gently toss to separate the noodles. Hang the noodles over a drying rack (see page 28) or the back of a clean chair to dry while you prep the remaining ingredients and the water comes to a boil. (Touching is okay but try not to overlap or clump the noodles.)

continued

Add the pasta to the water, stirring to separate it, and boil just until cooked through, about 90 seconds. Drain, reserving a bit of the cooking water. Place the noodles in a bowl with a bit of cool water mixed with a bit of the cooking water, just enough to coat but not submerge the noodles.

Prepare your fire for medium heat.

To make the ragù
Place a large cast-iron skillet over medium heat and pour in the oil. When it starts to smoke, add the leek, onion, and carrot. Cook until the vegetables start to brown and soften, then add the ground beef. Cook, stirring occasionally, until the beef is no longer pink. Stir in the tomato sauce and cook until heated through. Stir in the wine, oregano, salt, and pepper. Continue cooking until the wine reduces and you're left with a thick sauce. (A spoon dragged through it will leave a clear channel behind.)

Drop in the pasta, gently toss to coat, and cook until heated through. Serve with grated Parm and basil leaves.

NOT-SO-TRADITIONAL CARBONARA

What's so nontraditional about our carbonara? It's the garlic. We love it. You're not "supposed" to use it in carbonara, but it's in our veins! If you can't find smoked pork belly, choose pancetta or a fatty center-cut bacon.

DIRECTIONS

Prepare your fire for high heat. (If using a grill, set up one side for high heat and one side for medium heat.)

To make the pasta
Fill a large pot with 2 quarts (about 2 L) water, generously season the water with salt, and bring it to a boil over high heat.

Mound the flour on a large cutting board and create a well in the middle. Crack the eggs into the well and add the yolks, olive oil (if using), and a large pinch of salt. Using a fork, break up the eggs and gradually stir in the flour from the mound until all the flour is fully incorporated and you have a dry, craggy-looking dough ball (you might have to use your hands near the end). Knead until a smooth, stiff, yet pliable, dough ball forms, 8 to 10 minutes. Halve the dough.

Generously flour the cutting board and place the dough on it. Working with one half at a time, use a rolling pin to roll the dough very thin, so you can almost see your hand through it, about to the edges of your board, or 12 × 12 inches (30 × 30 cm) or so. Cut strips of dough, top to bottom, about 1/8 inch (0.3 cm) wide (see Forest Hack, page 59). Lightly sprinkle the noodles with flour and gently toss to separate them. Hang the noodles over a drying rack (see Bushrack, page 28) or the back of a clean chair to dry while the water comes to a boil and you prep the ingredients for the sauce. (Touching is okay but try not to overlap or clump the noodles.)

Add the pasta to the boiling water, stirring to separate the noodles, and boil just until cooked through, about 90 seconds. Drain, reserving a bit of the cooking water. Place the noodles in a bowl with a bit of cool water mixed with a bit of the cooking water, just enough to coat but not submerge the noodles.

Prepare your fire for medium heat.

continued

INGREDIENTS

For the pasta dough

Table salt

1 2/3 cups (200 g) all-purpose flour, plus more for dusting

2 large eggs

3 large egg yolks

1 tablespoon plus 1 teaspoon (20 ml) olive oil (optional)

For the sauce

About 11 ounces (300 g) smoked pork belly, diced

3 garlic cloves, sliced

1/2 cup (50 g) grated Parmesan cheese, plus 1 1/2 heaping tablespoons (9.5 g)

4 large egg yolks

1 teaspoon table salt

1 teaspoon ground black pepper

Handful of fresh parsley, chopped, plus more for garnish

1/2 teaspoon dried oregano

To make the sauce

Place the pork belly in a large cast-iron skillet over medium heat. Cook until it starts to brown and render its fat. Stir in the garlic and continue cooking until the pork and garlic are deep golden brown.

Place ½ cup (50 g) Parmesan in a medium bowl. Add the egg yolks and stir until well mixed.

Add the pasta to the skillet and toss to combine and coat with the fat. Gradually pour in the Parm-yolk mixture, a little at a time, stirring well after each addition, so the eggs don't scramble. Sprinkle with salt and pepper, toss, and remove from the heat.

Prepare your fire for medium-low heat.

Set a large cast-iron skillet over the lower heat and sprinkle the remaining 1½ heaping tablespoons (9.5 g) of Parmesan in an even layer. Sprinkle with a bit of parsley and the oregano. Cook until bubbling and starting to brown. (Push any straggler bits of cheese into the main mass to form a rough disk shape.) Let the skillet cool, and you'll be able to remove the crisp. (Or line the skillet with parchment paper before adding the cheese, and you'll be able to flip the cheese disk to make both sides golden.)

Serve the carbonara garnished with more chopped parsley and broken-up bits of the Parmesan crisp.

FOREST HACK

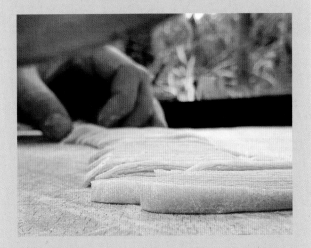

Here's an easy way to cut noodles evenly: Pick up either the top or bottom edge of the well-floured dough and fold it on itself, accordion style, folding back and forth four times, for a total of five layers. It will look like a neatly folded letter, the width of your board. To form the noodles, simply cut across the pleats every ⅛ inch (3 mm) or so.

FOREST LECZÓ (HUNGARIAN STEW)

Although this stew has Hungarian roots, different Eastern European countries put their own spins on it. To make this late-summer/early-fall vegetable stew more like how Slawek's mom made it, we use a smoked pork belly and smoked Polish sausage, which really taste amazing when cooked over an open fire. We also break with tradition by topping this stew with a sunny-side egg. We like the added pop of color, but feel free to skip it.

INGREDIENTS

About 11 ounces (300 g) smoked pork belly, skin removed, chopped

1 (5⅓-ounce, or 150 g) Polish sausage (smoked kielbasa), diced

1 yellow onion, finely diced

4 garlic cloves, sliced

3 bell peppers (a mix of colors), cut into strips

2 large tomatoes, diced

1 medium zucchini, diced

1⅔ cups (400 g) tomato sauce

1 teaspoon dried marjoram, plus more as needed

1 teaspoon paprika, plus more as needed

1 teaspoon table salt, plus more as needed

1 teaspoon ground black pepper, plus more as needed

3 or 4 dried bay leaves

4 large eggs (optional)

Chopped fresh parsley for garnish

DIRECTIONS

Prepare your fire for medium-high heat.

In a large pot over medium-high heat, combine the pork belly and sausage. Cook until they start to brown and render their fat, then add the onion and garlic and cook until softened and brown. You can lower the heat to medium at this point.

Add the vegetables, tomato sauce, spices, and bay leaves. Stir well and let the mixture bubble away until the vegetables are very soft and the stew is thick, 60 to 90 minutes. Taste for seasoning and remove from the heat. Remove and discard the bay leaves.

If using the eggs, place a large cast-iron skillet over medium heat and fry them to your liking, seasoned with salt and pepper. Top each bowl of stew with one egg and sprinkle with parsley.

CRUNCHY FRIED CAMEMBERT

This snack belongs in the "around the world" chapter because it's our typical mishmash of cuisines. There's the French cheese, of course, but the sauce we've created is a little bit like the Southeast Asian condiment sambal oelek and the North African sauce harissa—naturally, with our twist on it. It's spicy, tangy, and sweet—just the thing to cut through the fatty richness of the fried cheese. Interestingly, "oelek" is a colonialized adaptation of the word *ulek*, a device that's similar to a mortar and pestle. (Remember when we said everything tastes better when made that way?)

DIRECTIONS

Prepare your fire for high heat.

Use a mortar and pestle to mash together the green and red chiles, onion, garlic, ginger, and half the mint until broken up and pasty. Add the lime juice, tomato paste, honey, oil, 1 teaspoon salt, and pepper and mix well, stirring in the remaining mint. (If you don't have a mortar and pestle, combine everything in a food processor and pulse a few times.) Set aside.

In a shallow bowl, lightly beat the egg. In another shallow bowl (or on your cutting board), stir together the bread crumbs, parsley, paprika, and a generous pinch of salt. Place the flour in another bowl or elsewhere on your board.

Dust each wedge of cheese in the flour, coating all sides. Dip the cheese in the egg, allowing the excess to drip off, then coat in the bread crumbs.

In a large cast-iron skillet over high heat, pour in enough oil to reach a depth of about 1 inch (2.5 cm) When hot (see Forest Hack, below), add half the coated cheese wedges. Fry until golden on all sides and the cheese is properly gooey. Remove from the oil, repeat with the remaining wedges, and serve with the chile sauce, sprinkled with more parsley, if desired.

FOREST HACK

If your oil isn't hot enough, it will turn your cheese into a grease bomb. If it's too hot, it will burn the coating before the cheese melts. Ideally, you want your oil to be between 330°F and 340°F (165°C to 170°C) for this dish. To see if it's ready, flick some flour or bread crumbs into it. If it bubbles up immediately, it's good to go.

INGREDIENTS

2 fresh green chiles, thinly sliced (seeds retained for more heat)

2 fresh red chiles, thinly sliced

½ yellow onion, finely diced

3 garlic cloves, peeled

1- to 2-inch (2.5 to 5 cm) piece fresh ginger, peeled and finely chopped

Small handful of fresh mint leaves

Juice of ½ lime

2½ tablespoons (40 g) tomato paste

2 tablespoons (40 g) honey

2 tablespoons (30 ml) olive oil

Table salt

1 teaspoon ground black pepper

1 large egg

1 cup (115 g) dried bread crumbs

Handful of coarsely chopped fresh parsley, plus more for serving (optional)

1 teaspoon paprika

1¼ cups (150 g) all-purpose flour

2 (about 9-ounce, or 250 g) wheels Camembert cheese, each cut into 8 wedges

Oil for frying

MEAT MADNESS

If your idea of meat cooked over a fire involves a hot dog or a plain old burger that you flip ten times until it's a dried-out puck, then prepare yourself for something spectacular. In this chapter, we present life-changing recipes for a variety of mouthwatering steaks, pork ribs and sticky pork belly, even lamb chops smothered in a luscious pomegranate sauce. Cooking meat over a fire is almost primal, in some regards, so we're not messing around here.

NO-MESSING-ABOUT SKEWERS

Sure, anyone can cook food on a stick over a fire, but slathering kebabs with our cheese sauce is next level. As with the other recipes in this book, these skewers don't need to be "perfect." If you run out of red bell pepper before you finish making the last one, it's okay! You don't like zucchini? Leave it out! Remember, you're enjoying a wonderful day in the forest, so use what *you* like best. (But, if it's in your nature to have even-looking skewers, then you'll want eight pieces of each item.)

INGREDIENTS

For the skewers

4 garlic cloves, minced

2-inch (5 cm) piece fresh ginger, peeled and finely diced

2½ tablespoons (50 g) honey

2 tablespoons (30 ml) olive oil

2 tablespoons (30 ml) teriyaki sauce

2 tablespoons (30 ml) soy sauce

1 tablespoon ground black pepper

2 chicken breasts, cut into 1-inch (2.5 cm) pieces

2 (about 8-ounce, or 225 g) sirloin steaks, cut into 1-inch (2.5 cm) pieces

7 ounces (200 g) smoked pork belly, cut into 1 × 2-inch (2.5 × 5 cm) pieces

2 red bell peppers, cut into 2-inch (5 cm) pieces

1 small pineapple, peeled, cored, half cut into 2-inch (5 cm) pieces (snack on the other half!)

3 small red onions, quartered through the root (cut from the top down, not across the equator)

1 small to medium zucchini, sliced about ½ inch (1 cm) thick

For the cheese sauce

3 tablespoons plus 1 teaspoon (50 g) butter

¼ cup (30 g) all-purpose flour

½ cup plus 2 tablespoons (150 ml) milk

5½ ounces (100 g) orange, yellow, and/or white cheddar cheese, grated

1 teaspoon table salt, plus more as needed

1 teaspoon ground black pepper, plus more as needed

Chopped fresh parsley for garnish

DIRECTIONS

Prepare your fire for medium heat.

To make the skewers

In a large bowl, stir together the garlic, ginger, honey, oil, teriyaki sauce, soy sauce, and pepper.

Add the chicken, steak, and pork belly to the bowl and toss to coat the meat in the marinade. Let marinate while you prepare the remaining ingredients (the longer the better).

On skewers, thread a piece of bell pepper, pork belly, pineapple, chicken, onion, beef, and zucchini (basically, alternating produce and protein, but you do it however you like). Repeat the sequence again, for two pieces of everything per skewer. Set the skewers over the fire, basting with any remaining marinade and turning occasionally. (Once you baste, you have to turn it to cook that marinade because it had raw chicken in it. Skip the baste if this makes you nervous.) Cook until everything is nicely charred or browned and the chicken is thoroughly cooked through, 10 to 15 minutes—how long will depend on the conditions and the fuel you use (see Forest Hack, page 68).

continued

BUSHCRAFT
Make Your Own Skewers and Holder

Sure, you can buy skewers (especially if you're using a grill), but good luck finding the mammoth ones we use in this recipe! As you can imagine, we like to whittle our own. And if you're going to make your own skewers, you're going to need something to hold them over the fire. Here's how:

1. Find four thin, straight branches of equal size, a good 16 to 18 inches (40 to 45 cm)—with at least a couple inches (about 5 cm) overhang on both ends from where they'll rest in the skewer holder.

2. Whittle off any errant smaller branches and strip the main branch of bark.

3. Sharpen one end of each branch.

4. Re-create the setup for the Two-Pan Holder on page 101. (It doesn't have to be nearly as strong, but the cross-branches should be about 1 inch, or 2.5 cm, in diameter.)

5. In one cross-branch, use your knife to cut out four V-shaped notches, a couple inches (about 5 cm) apart. The notches just have to be deep enough to hold the skewers. Do the same on the other cross-branch, making the notches at about the same place as on the first branch—it doesn't have to be perfect!

6. Don't set the cross-branches in the holders until you're ready to thread the skewers.

To make the cheese sauce
In a large cast-iron skillet over medium heat, melt the butter. A little at a time, stir in the flour until it's all incorporated and a thick paste forms; cook for 1 minute before pouring in the milk. Cook, stirring, until any lumps are gone. When thicken and bubbling, add the cheese and cook until melted and smooth. Stir in the salt and pepper and taste for seasoning. Pour the sauce over the kebabs and sprinkle with parsley to serve.

FOREST HACK

You want enough heat to cook your food, but not so much that it burns through the very thing that's holding up your food—that is, a wooden skewer. It's all well and good to use what we find in the forest to cook our meals, but what we've found with recipes like this one is that charcoal briquettes can be a dinner saver. Charcoal gives you constant heat without the fickle flame that wood does. If the flame's not burning your food, it's not burning your skewers. And less messing about with the flame means more time spent enjoying yourself.

TOMAHAWK STEAK

A tomahawk steak is what happens to rib eye when it dresses up for a night out. It has a good 5 inches (13 cm) of rib bone that's French trimmed, making a sort of handle. The steak is easily 1 to 2 inches (2.5 to 5 cm) thick, and it's probably going to be larger than your 12-inch (30 cm) skillet. For that reason, we use a cast-iron griddle pan (they're usually about 10 × 17 inches or 19 inches, or 25 × 40 cm or 48 cm) and set it over the fire using the Two-Pan setup on page 101. Because this recipe is dressed up, we serve it with cocktail tomatoes, which are small (like cherry tomatoes) and usually come in clusters, with their stems intact. They're easy to add to and remove from the pan, and they look nice! Use whatever tomatoes you like.

DIRECTIONS

Prepare your fire for high heat.

In a small bowl, mash the butter until pliable. Add the garlic, parsley, table salt, and ground pepper and mash until well combined and very soft. Form into five large spoonfuls (see How to Make Quenelles Like a French Chef, page 71).

Set the steak on your cutting board and generously season all sides with sea salt and cracked pepper, rubbing it in a bit.

Place a griddle pan over high heat and pour in the oil. When smoking, set the steak on its edge (bone-side down) and sear until it forms a golden-brown crust. (You might have to hold it up.) Sear all the remaining edges before setting the steak on its side. When a golden crust develops, flip the steak onto its final side. Place two spoonfuls of butter on the steak and add two to the griddle, along with the rosemary and thyme. Where there's space, add the tomatoes.

INGREDIENTS

1¼ cups (1½ sticks) plus 1 tablespoon plus 1 teaspoon (200 g) butter, at room temperature

5 garlic cloves, thinly sliced

Small handful of fresh parsley, chopped

1 teaspoon table salt

1 teaspoon ground black pepper

1 tomahawk steak (1½ inches, or 3.5 cm)

Flaky sea salt

Freshly cracked black pepper

1 to 2 tablespoons (15 to 30 ml) olive oil

2 or 3 rosemary sprigs

3 or 4 thyme sprigs

2 "stems" cocktail tomatoes (10 to 12 tomatoes)

1 loaf ciabatta, sliced about 1 inch (2.5 cm) thick

continued

HOW TO MAKE QUENELLES LIKE A FRENCH CHEF

Just because we're in the forest doesn't mean we can't be upscale. A quenelle is just a tidier version of a spoonful. (Though, to be honest, we still use camp sporks to make these!) Here's how you make one:

1. Using a spoon, scoop one spoonful of the butter mixture.

2. Holding a second spoon of the same size in your other hand, scoop the butter from the first spoon onto the second spoon.

3. Repeat five or six times. Each time you do this, rotate the butter a bit, so the sides start to smooth out, and it begins to take on an oval shape.

Cook the steak to your liking, about 15 minutes for medium to medium-rare, periodically basting it with the butter and juices. (This will smell amazing, by the way!)

Transfer the steak and tomatoes to a cutting board to rest and top the steak with the remaining spoonful of butter. Place the bread on the griddle and cook until lightly charred on both sides.

Slice the steak and serve it on the bread with the tomatoes.

SIRLOIN STEAK WITH HASSELBACK POTATOES

Sirloin steaks are a breeze to cook over an open fire—they're fast and flavorful. Hasselback potatoes look complicated but are actually quite easy to make. Simply slice the potato cross-wise, making the cuts about $\frac{1}{16}$ inch (0.16 cm) apart and about halfway through to the bottom. You want to keep the potato whole. (This also works on other veggies like eggplant, zucchini, even carrots.)

INGREDIENTS

For the potatoes

About 1 pound, 2 ounces (500 g) baby potatoes (such as Yukon gold), "hasselbacked"

3 tablespoons plus 1 teaspoon (50 ml) olive oil

1 to 2 teaspoons lemon pepper

1 to 2 teaspoons table salt

2 to 3 teaspoons mixed spices (cayenne pepper, garlic powder, oregano, paprika)

1 rosemary sprig, leaves removed

4 garlic cloves, peeled

3 tablespoons plus 1 teaspoon (50 g) butter

For the steak

1 (1-inch, or 2.5 cm, -thick) sirloin steak (figure 6 to 8 ounces, or 170 to 225 g, per person)

Flaky sea salt

Freshly cracked black pepper

2 tablespoons (30 ml) oil

2 tablespoons (30 g) butter

4 garlic cloves, peeled

3 or 4 rosemary sprigs

3 or 4 thyme sprigs

For the mustard sauce

1 tablespoon (15 ml) oil

2 shallots, finely chopped

$\frac{1}{2}$ cup plus 2 tablespoons (150 ml) heavy cream

1 tablespoon (15 g) whole-grain mustard

1 tablespoon (6 g) grated lemon zest, plus more as needed

1 teaspoon table salt, plus more as needed

1 teaspoon ground black pepper, plus more as needed

DIRECTIONS

Prepare your fire for medium heat. (If using a grill, set up one side for high heat and one side for medium heat.)

To make the potatoes

In a large bowl, combine the potatoes, oil, lemon pepper, table salt, spices, and rosemary. Toss to coat and combine, then pour the ingredients into a large cast-iron skillet over medium heat and add the garlic and butter to melt.

Turn the potatoes cut-side down and cook until golden. Turn the potatoes over and cover with an inverted skillet (or close the grill lid). Place a large handful of coals on top, covering the whole thing. Cook until tender inside and crispy outside, about 20 minutes, while you prepare the remaining ingredients. Replenish the coals as needed.

Prepare your fire for high heat.

continued

To make the steak
Generously season all sides of the steak (including the edges) with sea salt and cracked pepper, pressing the spices into the meat.

Pour the oil into a second (or clean) large cast-iron skillet over high heat. When smoking, add the steak, searing it on the fatty edge (you might have to hold it up) before setting it on its side and cooking until a deep golden crust develops. Flip the steak and add the butter, garlic, rosemary, and thyme to the skillet. Cook, periodically basting the steak with the butter and juices, until done to your liking,

2½ to 3 minutes per side. Transfer to a cutting board to rest while you prepare the mustard sauce.

To make the mustard sauce
Clean the skillet, return it to the heat, pour in the oil, and add the shallots. Cook until lightly browned and softened. Add the cream, mustard, lemon zest, table salt, and ground pepper. Cook, stirring, until thickened and bubbling. Taste for seasoning and remove from heat.

To serve, slice the steak, spooning the mustard sauce over. Devour with the potatoes.

MASSIVE RUMP STEAK

Rump steaks are, as their name suggests, from the hind end of the cow, farther back than the sirloin. Because it's farther back (and gets worked more), it's a bit tougher, a bit more inexpensive, and, some might say, more flavorful. Although the savory butter baste will help tenderize this cut, do ask your butcher to tenderize it, and be sure to give it a good rest after cooking and before slicing into it.

DIRECTIONS

Prepare your fire for high heat.

Place a grill pan over high heat.

Generously season both sides of the steak with salt and pepper, pressing the spices into the meat.

Pour 2 tablespoons (30 ml) oil into the hot pan. When smoking, add the steak and cook until a nice golden crust forms. Flip the steak and add the whole garlic, thyme, rosemary, and butter. Cook, periodically basting the steak with the butter and juices, until done to your liking, about 7 minutes per side. Give the fatty edge a quick sear before transferring the steak to a cutting board to rest while you make the sauce.

Using a mortar and pestle, mash the onion, bell pepper, sliced garlic, remaining 2 tablespoons (30 ml) of oil, 1 teaspoon salt, and 1 teaspoon pepper until an emulsified sauce develops. Stir in the parsley. (If you don't have a mortar and pestle, combine the ingredients in a food processor and pulse a few times.)

Slice the steak and spoon the sauce over it.

INGREDIENTS

1½ to 2 pounds (700 to 800 g) rump steak

Flaky sea salt

Freshly cracked black pepper

4 tablespoons (60 ml) olive oil, divided

8 garlic cloves, 4 whole and 4 sliced

Couple thyme sprigs

Couple rosemary sprigs

3 tablespoons plus 1 teaspoon (50 g) butter

1 small red onion, finely chopped

1 red bell pepper, finely chopped

Small handful of fresh parsley, chopped

FRIED STEAK

Here, we call for "frying steak," what some might call "minute steak," which can be cut from anywhere on the cow, but often comes from the flank, strip, or sirloin. You want the steak thinly cut, about ½ inch (1 cm) thick, so it cooks quickly. Minute steaks are typically flash-fried and served with some sort of gravy. Although that approach can be great on a busy weeknight, we like to take our time out here in the forest to create something a bit more special.

INGREDIENTS

For the steak

2 (5⅓-ounce, or 150 g) frying steaks

3 tablespoons, plus 1 teaspoon (50 ml) balsamic vinegar, divided

Paprika for seasoning

Table salt

Ground black pepper

6 thin spears asparagus, woody ends trimmed

3 bell peppers, a mix of colors, 2 thin strips cut from each, and the rest diced

1 red onion, half finely diced, half sliced

2 tablespoons (30 ml) oil

2 medium to large portobello mushrooms, stemmed

4 garlic cloves, sliced

1 teaspoon ground cumin

1 teaspoon dried oregano

For the sauce

4 garlic cloves, peeled

½ teaspoon ground black pepper

Small handful of fresh mint leaves

2 tablespoons (30 ml) olive oil

6 tablespoons plus 2 teaspoons (100 g) plain yogurt

Grated lemon zest for seasoning

1 tablespoon (15 ml) fresh lemon juice

DIRECTIONS

Prepare your fire for medium heat.

To make the steaks

Set the steaks on a cutting board and drizzle with 1 teaspoon vinegar, rubbing it into the meat. Generously season the steaks with paprika, salt, and pepper. Place three asparagus spears, three bell pepper slices, and a few onion slices horizontally on each steak, near one end. Roll up the steaks around the vegetables and run a skewer through the flap to secure the rolls. (We whittle our own skewers, but you probably guessed that already!)

Place a large cast-iron skillet over medium heat and pour in the oil. When shimmering, add the steak rolls, skewer/seam-side down to the skillet, along with the mushrooms, gill-side up. Cook until both are deeply golden brown, then flip. Cover with an inverted skillet (no need for coals here; or close the grill lid), and cook until golden brown and cooked through, 8 to 10 minutes. Remove from the skillet.

Add the diced bell peppers and onion and the garlic to the skillet, along with the remaining 3 tablespoons (45 ml) of vinegar, cumin, oregano, 1 teaspoon salt, and 1 teaspoon pepper. Stir to combine and cook until the vinegar has evaporated and the veggies are al dente. Remove the skillet from the heat.

To make the sauce

Use a mortar and pestle to mash the garlic, pepper, and mint into a paste. Pour in the oil and stir in the yogurt, lemon zest to taste, and lemon juice until well combined. (If you don't have a mortar and pestle, combine the ingredients in a food processor and pulse a few times.)

To serve, top the portobellos with the cooked veggie mixture. Remove the skewers from the beef and cut the rolls in half, spooning the yogurt sauce over the top.

PERFECT T-BONE STEAK

For the potatoes in this recipe, we use a Polish potato seasoning called *przyprawa do ziemniakow*. This mixture of spices (such as caraway, coriander, dill, garlic, lemon zest, marjoram, onion, and paprika) comes in a packet and is specifically for potatoes—similar to those packets for French onion soup mix or ranch dressing mix. Depending on where you are, you can find *przyprawa do ziemniakow* in stores (we found it in a Polish market here in Ireland), but, as always, use whatever spices you have or like on potatoes. We think the bit of lemon zest in this blend tastes nice; it breaks through the rich, fatty meat.

DIRECTIONS

Prepare your fire for high heat. (If using a grill, set up one side for high heat and one side for medium heat.)

Put half the butter in a camp cup and set it next to your fire while you gather your ingredients. (Or put it in a saucepan and set it on the medium-heat side of the grill.)

In a large bowl, toss the potatoes with 1 tablespoon oil, the potato seasoning, table salt, and ground pepper to coat.

To the melted butter, add the sliced garlic, parsley, a generous pinch of sea salt, and cracked pepper. Set aside.

Generously season the steak on all sides (including the edges!) with sea salt and cracked pepper, rubbing the spices in a bit.

Place a grill pan over high heat and pour in the remaining 1 tablespoon (15 ml) of oil. When smoking, add the steak, searing it on the fatty edge (you might have to hold it up) before setting it on its side and cooking until a deep golden crust and nice dark grill marks develop. Flip the steak and carefully pour the whisky into the pan—it will likely ignite! (If you're using a gas grill, or this otherwise worries you, remove the pan from the flame before adding the whisky, then return it to the heat.)

Let the whisky burn off until the pan is almost dry, then add the remaining butter, along with the thyme, rosemary, and whole garlic. Cook, periodically basting the steak with the butter and juices, until done to your liking, 3 to 4 minutes per side. (Pay attention to the filet because it will cook faster than the sirloin.) Transfer to a cutting board to rest while you cook the potatoes.

Prepare your fire for medium heat.

Add the potatoes and tomatoes to the skillet, cooking until the potatoes are crispy and have nice grill marks on both sides, 4 to 5 minutes.

Slice the steak (see How to Carve a T-Bone Like a Boss, page 80), and spoon over the garlic-parsley butter. Serve a steak slice on a potato, with tomatoes for garnish.

INGREDIENTS

½ cup (1 stick) plus 2 tablespoons (150 g) butter, divided

2 medium potatoes, thinly sliced

2 tablespoons (30 ml) olive oil, divided

2 teaspoons potato seasoning (*przyprawa do ziemniakow*)

1 teaspoon table salt

1 teaspoon ground black pepper

9 garlic cloves, 5 sliced, 4 left whole

Handful of fresh parsley, finely chopped

Flaky sea salt

Freshly cracked black pepper

1 (1-inch, or 2.5 cm, -thick) T-bone steak

½ cup plus 2 tablespoons (150 ml) whisky

Few thyme sprigs

Few rosemary sprigs

Cocktail tomatoes for presentation

HOW TO CARVE A T-BONE LIKE A BOSS

A T-bone consists of two steaks: a strip of top loin (the longer side) and a bit of tenderloin (where filet mignon comes from). To keep from fighting over who gets what, slice it the way the pros do, then everyone can share. Here's how:

1. Set the steak upright, with the "T" upside-down. Cut along the bone from the top all the way to the bottom, removing the meat as one piece from the bone.

2. Repeat on the other side.

3. Slice each steak crosswise.

4. To present, reassemble the slices along the bone, so it resembles the original T-bone steak.

TROPICAL PORK RIBS

We originally called these "Polish-style ribs with *wódka*"—Polish style *because* of the vodka. But, honestly, we never heard of anyone cooking ribs with this spirit, and we wanted to do something a little different. People were surprised, but the response was good! We think a little adventure with pork ribs never hurt anybody, so we hope you'll give it a try.

DIRECTIONS

Prepare your fire for medium heat.

Generously season the ribs on all side with salt and pepper, pressing the spices into the meat.

Place a large cast-iron skillet over medium heat and pour in the oil. When shimmering, add the ribs and cook until a deep golden crust forms. Flip the ribs and sear the other side until you get a nice color on them. Remove the ribs from the skillet (they won't be cooked through at this point).

In the skillet, combine the onion and garlic halves, cut-side down. Cook until the onion begins to brown and soften, then add the chiles, mango, and pineapple, stirring to combine. Cook until everything's a little bit caramelized, 7 to 10 minutes.

Carefully pour in the vodka—it will likely ignite! (If you're using a gas grill, or this otherwise worries you, remove the skillet from the flame before adding the vodka, then return it to the heat. Our hands are like ice cubes, so we don't really feel the flames!) Let it burn down until the pan is nearly dry and the vegetables are tender.

Set the ribs on top of the veggies and drizzle the honey over the ribs. Add a splash more vodka, cover with an inverted skillet, and place a large handful of coals on top (or close the grill lid). Let your fire go low at this point and cook until the ribs are cooked through and the veggies are almost jammy, 15 to 20 minutes, replenishing the coals as needed.

Spoon the veggies over the ribs and sprinkle with chives and sesame seeds before tearing into them.

continued

INGREDIENTS

1¾ pounds (800 g) pork rib tips, cut into 4 pieces

Flaky sea salt

Freshly cracked black pepper

2 tablespoons (30 ml) olive oil

1 yellow onion, halved and sliced

1 head garlic, halved crosswise

3 fresh red chiles, thinly sliced (seeds retained for more heat)

1 mango, peeled and diced (see page 83)

1 small pineapple, peeled, cored, half diced (snack on the other half; see page 88)

1¼ cups (300 ml) vodka, plus a splash

Scant ½ cup (150 g) honey

Chopped fresh chives for garnish

Sesame seeds for garnish

HOW TO PEEL A MANGO LIKE YOU KNOW WHAT YOU'RE DOING

Sure, you can use a vegetable peeler to peel your mango, but did you really pack it for your trip to the forest? There's a simpler way. Here's how:

1. Cut down the long sides of the mango—there's a large pit in the middle, so get as close to that pit as you can.

2. On the flesh side of the pieces you cut off, use the tip of your knife to cut a cross-hatch pattern. Don't cut all the way through the skin, just far enough to cut through the fruit.

3. Flex the skin, like you're trying to turn it inside-out, and all the little cubes of mango will stand out. You can either pluck them off or cut them off at the base.

4. To get the remaining mango, cut along the edges of the pit, then run your knife between the flesh and the skin.

PINEAPPLE PORK

When we set out to make this dish, a massive rain cloud came in from nowhere and stuck with us for a good 40 minutes. We kept at it, though, because it takes us a lot of time to find the right spot and chop the wood. And once we prepare the ingredients, there's nothing to do but see it through. We're glad we did because this meal turned out fantastic!

INGREDIENTS

1 (about 14-ounce, or 400 g) pork tenderloin, trimmed

Table salt

Ground black pepper

2 tablespoons (30 g) butter or (30 ml) oil

5 or 6 (½-inch, or 0.6 cm, -thick) pineapple slices, halved

Large red bell pepper, finely chopped

2 fresh chiles (different colors, if desired), thinly sliced (seeds retained for more heat)

1 red onion, finely diced

1¼ cups (300 ml) pineapple juice

2½ tablespoons (50 g) honey

2 tablespoons (32 g) barbecue sauce

1 teaspoon paprika

1 teaspoon garlic powder

1 spring onion, sliced

DIRECTIONS

Prepare your fire for medium heat. (If using a grill, set up one side for medium heat and one side for low/indirect heat.)

Generously season all sides of the pork with salt and pepper.

In a large cast-iron skillet over medium heat, melt the butter. Add the pork to the skillet and sear all sides until deeply golden brown. Remove from the heat. Cut into the sides of the tenderloin, about 1 inch (2.5 cm) apart but not all the way through. Insert a pineapple slice into each cut (they will stick out of the top).

In a large bowl, stir together the bell pepper, chiles, onion, pineapple juice, honey, barbecue sauce, paprika, garlic powder, 1 teaspoon salt, and 1 teaspoon pepper.

Wipe out the skillet, return the pork to it, and place it over medium heat. Spoon a couple spoonfuls of the pepper sauce over the pork, then pour the rest of the sauce into the skillet. Bring to a boil, cover the skillet with an inverted skillet, and top with a large handful of coals, nearly covering the entire thing—this will lower the heat, which is fine, as you don't want a lot of heat from below. (If using a grill, move to low/indirect heat and close the grill lid.) Cook until the pork is cooked through to your liking and the sauce is thickened, 30 to 35 minutes, replenishing the coals as needed.

Remove the pork from the skillet and slice (we recommend down the middle). Spoon over more sauce and sprinkle with spring onion before devouring.

STICKY PORK BELLY

Pork belly and whisky—together at last! This recipe came about because we always wanted to make pork belly, and we wanted to make a recipe with whisky. It's as simple as that. Whisky might not be a common ingredient in sticky pork belly, but we love how the flavor blends with the ginger and honey in the sauce.

DIRECTIONS

Prepare your fire for medium-low heat.

Use a mortar and pestle to mash the garlic, ginger, chile, peppercorns, and salt into a paste. Pour in the oil, honey, and soy sauce and stir to combine. (If you don't have a mortar and pestle, combine the ingredients in a food processor and pulse a few times.) Set aside.

Place a large cast-iron skillet over medium-low heat. When hot, add the pork. Cook until browned on all sides and the fat starts to render. Carefully pour in the whisky—it will likely ignite! (If you're using a gas grill, or this otherwise worries you, remove the skillet from the flame before adding the whiskey, then return it to the heat.) Continue to burn off the whisky, then pour in the garlic-ginger sauce. Cook, uncovered, until the sauce is thick and glossy and the pork is cooked through, 60 to 90 minutes.

Serve garnished with sesame seeds and fresh parsley.

INGREDIENTS

4 garlic cloves, sliced

2-inch (5 cm) piece fresh ginger, peeled and finely diced

1 fresh red chile, finely diced (seeds retained for more heat)

½ teaspoon peppercorns

½ teaspoon flaky sea salt

6 tablespoons plus 2 teaspoons (100 ml) olive oil

2½ tablespoons (50 g) honey

3 tablespoons plus 1 teaspoon (50 ml) soy sauce

1 (2¼-pound, about 1 kg) slab pork belly cut into 1-inch (2.5 cm) cubes

1⅔ cups (400 ml) whisky

Sesame seeds for garnish

Chopped fresh parsley or snipped fresh chives for garnish

SWEET PINEAPPLE BEEF

If you liked the Sticky Pork Belly (page 87), you're going to *love* this Sweet Pineapple Beef. (But you can also use pork tenderloin or thin-cut pork chops here!) If you want to kick up your presentation, get a second pineapple and cut it through the middle from top to bottom. Scoop or cut out the center, leaving about 1/2 inch (1 cm) around the edges—and voilà: a pineapple boat.

INGREDIENTS

1 cup (200 g) short-grain white rice

Table salt

1 tablespoon (15 g) coconut oil

About 11 ounces (300 g) frying (or "minute") steaks, cut into ½-inch (1 cm) pieces

1 yellow onion, finely chopped

½ pineapple, peeled, cored, and cubed (see below)

1 red bell pepper, diced

1 yellow bell pepper, diced

4 garlic cloves, sliced

1-inch (2.5 cm) piece fresh ginger, peeled and finely diced

2 tablespoons plus 2 teaspoons (40 g) brown sugar

1 tablespoon plus 1 teaspoon (20 ml) soy sauce

1 teaspoon ground black pepper

1 spring onion, sliced

Sesame seeds for garnish

DIRECTIONS

Prepare your fire for medium heat.

In a large cast-iron pot, combine the rice and a good pinch of salt. Pour in enough water to cover the rice by about ¾ inch (1.5 cm). Cover the pot with a tight-fitting lid and set it over medium heat. Cook until the water is absorbed, 15 to 20 minutes. Meanwhile, prepare the remaining ingredients.

In a large cast-iron skillet over medium heat, melt the oil. Add the steaks and cook until brown on all sides. Add the onion and cook until tender, a few minutes more. Add the pineapple, bell peppers, garlic, ginger, brown sugar, soy sauce, 1 teaspoon salt, and the pepper. Stir well and cook until the veggies are tender, 10 to 12 minutes.

Serve the steak and vegetables with the rice, sprinkled with the spring onion and sesame seeds.

HOW TO PEEL AND CORE A PINEAPPLE IN A FLASH

You don't need a fancy gadget to peel and core a pineapple— just a sharp knife. Here's how:

1. Set the pineapple on its side and cut off the top and bottom.

2. Set the pineapple on its base and run your knife just under the skin from top to bottom. (If there are any eyes left, cut those off, too.)

3. You'll be able to see the circular core. Just cut from the top down on either side of it, creating two large halves. Then, cut the remaining smaller sides from the core.

4. Slice or chop as needed.

LAMB CHOPS WITH POMEGRANATE SAUCE

This was one of those dishes that we weren't sure would work. Someone had asked us to make lamb, which we don't often cook, but the pomegranate sauce turned out quite nice, and the result is one tasty dish. If lamb's not your thing, filet mignon would make an amazing substitute.

DIRECTIONS

Prepare your fire for medium to high heat. (If using a grill, set up one side for high heat and one side for medium heat.)

Fill a large pot with 2 quarts (about 2 L) water, generously season the water with salt, and bring it to a boil over high heat. Add the potatoes and boil until tender, about 25 minutes. Meanwhile, prep the remaining ingredients.

Prepare your fire for medium heat.

Generously season the lamb chops on both sides with salt and pepper, pressing the spices into the meat.

Set a grill pan over medium heat and pour in 1 tablespoon (15 ml) oil. When shimmering, add the lamb chops and place a thyme sprig on top of each. Cook until a deeply golden crust forms, then flip. Add the butter and rosemary to the pan. Cook, periodically basting the lamb chops with the butter and juices, until done to your liking, 4 to 5 minutes per side. Transfer to a cutting board to rest, covering to keep warm, while you make the sauce and finish the potatoes. Clean the grill pan.

In a skillet over medium heat, combine the pomegranate arils, remaining thyme sprig, red wine, oregano, 1 teaspoon salt, and 1 teaspoon pepper. Cook until thickened and saucy, 15 to 20 minutes (the pom seeds are quite juicy!), then remove from the heat.

Return the clean grill pan to medium heat and pour in the remaining 1 tablespoon (15 ml) of oil. Drain the potatoes and place them in the grill pan. Sprinkle with salt, pepper, and paprika. Cook until golden grill marks develop, then flip and season the other side as you did the first, cooking until you have nice grill marks.

Serve the lamb, drizzled with the sauce, alongside the potatoes.

INGREDIENTS

Table salt

2 medium potatoes, thickly sliced (½ inch, or 1 cm)

Ground black pepper

3 bone-in lamb chops

2 tablespoons (30 ml) olive oil, divided

4 thyme sprigs

¼ cup (½ stick, or 60 g) butter

2 rosemary sprigs

1 pomegranate, arils removed

¾ cup plus 1 tablespoon plus 1 teaspoon (200 ml) red wine

1 teaspoon dried oregano

Paprika for seasoning

CAMPFIRE IRISH STEW

When we first made this recipe, we were both working in hotels, so this is a special stew we created for our Irish brothers and sisters at that time. We keep it very simple, but we make it with Guinness. It's the perfect meal for one of those colder days out in the forest.

INGREDIENTS

About 14 ounces (400 g) boneless lamb steaks (thin-cut), cut into 1-inch (2.5 cm) pieces

3 garlic cloves, sliced

¾ cup plus 1 tablespoon plus 1 teaspoon (200 ml) beef broth

3 celery stalks, sliced ¼ to ½ inch (0.6 to 1 cm) thick

1 white or yellow onion, coarsely chopped

1 large carrot, sliced into ¼- to ½-inch (0.6 to 1 cm) coins

1 cup (240 ml) red wine

1 cup (240 ml) Guinness

4 dried bay leaves

6 whole allspice berries

1 tablespoon dried parsley

1 teaspoon table salt

1 teaspoon ground black pepper

2 medium potatoes, peeled and chopped into ½- to 1-inch (1 to 2.5 cm) pieces

Chopped fresh parsley for garnish

DIRECTIONS

Prepare your fire for medium heat.

Place a large well-seasoned pot over medium heat. Add the lamb and cook until browned. Add the garlic and cook for 1 minute, pour in the broth, and bring it to a boil. Stir in the celery, onion, and carrot.

Carefully add the wine, Guinness, bay leaves, and spices. Cover the pot and cook until the lamb and vegetables are tender, 30 to 40 minutes.

Add the potatoes, re-cover the pot, and cook until tender, 15 to 20 minutes more. Serve, sprinkled with chopped fresh parsley.

BUSHCRAFT
Make Your Own Tripod Potholder

For something that cooks a long time, like a stew, we prefer using a tripod, so there's no wood directly over or in the flame. Here's how:

1. As its name suggests, you'll need three relatively straight branches of equal size, 5 to 6 feet (150 to 180 cm) long. You'll also need a fourth branch, not quite that length, with some smaller branches on one end of it.

2. Set the three main branches in a tripod. Hang the fourth, shorter branch from the middle—the end with the smaller branches on it goes at the top, so those branches can help anchor it to the tripod.

3. Lash them all together near the top with vines (or rope, if you prefer). Set them wide enough apart so there's plenty of space for your fire.

4. Use your handsaw to cut out a notch in the dangling branch where the handle of your pot will go. You'll want it positioned so the bottom of your pot will just be in the flames (for medium heat).

5. If the branch below the notch is too long, so it might get in the way of your cooking, cut that off, leaving a good 1 to 2 inches (2.5 to 5 cm) below the notch.

CHICKEN, TURKEY, AND DUCK

When we set out to make recipes for chicken, our main concern was that it can be quite boring, bland, and dry. Rest assured, these recipes are anything but! Here, we give you the best fried chicken you've ever tasted, the hottest chicken to ever curse your lips, and the prettiest chicken breast you've ever seen. And if you're looking for something extra special, or your palate is just feeling a bit more adventurous, we've added unique recipes for (not-dry) turkey and (not-greasy) duck. Poultry never had it so good!

FOREST-FRIED CHICKEN

You don't need to eat out to get the best fried chicken—you just need to make it *outdoors*. You can even make your own coleslaw while you're at it. We do like our food a bit on the spicy side, using the same amount of cayenne pepper as we do other spices, but if that's not your thing, scale back. And about that slaw: it can safely sit out (covered, if you wish) until the chicken is made, but if it's particularly hot outside, or you're at all concerned for food safety, put it your cooler.

INGREDIENTS

2 quarts (about 2 L) oil

For the coleslaw

¼ head cabbage, sliced

½ yellow onion, halved and sliced

1 carrot, julienned

3 tablespoons (45 g) mayonnaise

3 tablespoons (45 g) plain yogurt

2 teaspoons table salt

1 teaspoon ground black pepper

1 teaspoon grated orange zest

2 teaspoons fresh orange juice

2 teaspoons apple cider vinegar

Chopped fresh parsley for garnish

For the chicken

¾ cup plus 1 tablespoon plus
1 teaspoon (200 ml) buttermilk

2 teaspoons paprika, divided

2 teaspoons garlic powder, divided

2 teaspoons table salt, divided

2 teaspoons cayenne pepper, divided

3 chicken breasts

1²/₃ cups (200 g) all-purpose flour

1 teaspoon baking soda

1 teaspoon dried oregano

For the garlic sauce

5 garlic cloves, peeled

1 fresh chile, sliced (seeds retained for more heat)

1 tablespoon (4 g) fresh dill

1 teaspoon table salt

1 teaspoon ground black pepper

Chopped fresh parsley for garnish

1 teaspoon ground black pepper

3 tablespoons (45 g) plain yogurt

1½ tablespoons (30 g) honey

1 tablespoon (15 g) mayonnaise

Chopped fresh parsley for seasoning

DIRECTIONS

Prepare your fire for medium to high heat.

Pour the oil into a cast-iron pot and set it over the heat.

To make the slaw
In a large bowl, combine the cabbage, onion, carrot, mayonnaise, yogurt, salt, black pepper, orange zest, orange juice, and vinegar. Mix well to coat and combine and sprinkle with parsley. Set aside.

To make the chicken
In a large bowl, stir together the buttermilk, 1 teaspoon paprika, 1 teaspoon garlic powder, 1 teaspoon salt, and ½ to 1 teaspoon cayenne to taste. Halve the chicken lengthwise, making two thinner breasts. Submerge the chicken pieces in the buttermilk mixture. Set aside to marinate while you make the garlic sauce. (It is safe to set aside for a couple minutes, covered if you wish.)

To make the garlic sauce
Use a mortar and pestle to crush the garlic, chile, dill, salt, and black pepper into a paste. Add the yogurt, honey, mayonnaise, and a bit of chopped parsley, stirring until well combined. (If you don't have a mortar and pestle, combine the ingredients in a food processor and pulse a few times.) Set aside.

continued

To finish the chicken

When the oil is hot (see Forest Hack, at left), in a large bowl, stir together the flour, baking soda, oregano, black pepper, remaining 1 teaspoon of paprika, remaining 1 teaspoon of garlic powder, remaining 1 teaspoon of salt, and remaining 1 teaspoon of cayenne. Working in batches, remove a piece of chicken from the marinade, letting the excess drip off, and dredge it thoroughly in the seasoned flour before carefully adding to the hot oil—it will bubble furiously. Cook until the chicken is nice and golden and cooked through, about 12 minutes. (The deeply golden color of the batter is really the best indicator of doneness.) Remove from the oil.

Serve the chicken drizzled with the garlic sauce and sprinkled with parsley, alongside the slaw. You won't believe the crunch of that chicken!

HONEY MUSTARD CHICKEN QUARTERS

It's true: we enjoy cooking with alcohol—it tastes good and the pyrotechnics look great on film! But since we spend hours out in the forest—with fire—we can't really be *drinking* alcohol all day. We often choose a nonalcoholic brew for our dishes, and this recipe shows that you don't need any buzz to enjoy a great-tasting meal. We use two grill pans here to get those beautiful grill marks on the chicken and the veggies. Refer to Bushcraft, page 101, to see how we set it up.

INGREDIENTS

2 whole skin-on chicken legs (leg and thigh)

Flaky sea salt

Freshly cracked black pepper

1 teaspoon sweet paprika, plus more for the chicken

7 ounces (200 g) smoked pork belly, cut into ½-inch (1 cm) sticks (about the size of cheese sticks)

3½ ounces (100 g) king oyster mushrooms, halved lengthwise

1 small yellow onion, sliced ¼ inch (0.6 cm) thick (slice through the whole onion to make rings, but keep the rings together)

4 garlic cloves, peeled

1 (12-ounce, or 180 ml) bottle beer

2 teaspoons whole-grain mustard

1 teaspoon table salt

1 teaspoon ground black pepper

2½ tablespoons (50 g) honey

2 fresh chiles, sliced (seeds retained for more heat)

Few thyme sprigs

Chopped fresh parsley for garnish

DIRECTIONS

Prepare your fire for medium-high heat.

Generously season both sides of the chicken with sea salt, cracked pepper, and paprika.

Place two grill pans over medium-high heat. Place the chicken in one pan, skin-side up, and the pork belly in the other. Cook until golden brown, flipping the chicken a few times and stirring the pork to get all sides.

When the pork is nicely brown all over (while the chicken continues to cook), make room in the pork pan and add as many of the mushrooms and onions (as whole slices) as you can, along with the garlic. If there's not enough room, add some to the chicken pan. Cook until good grill marks form on the onion and mushrooms, then flip. Transfer the chicken to the pork skillet (along with any onions and mushrooms you may have put in there), setting the legs, skin-side up, on top on everything.

continued

BUSHCRAFT
Make Your Own Two-Pan Holder

1. Follow the directions for the Noodle Drying Rack on page 28, times two, skipping the whittling part. You want your sticks to be strong enough to hold two pans plus the ingredients.

2. Set up the "racks" on either side of your fire, wide enough apart so the handles of the pans can rest on the cross-branches.

3. Don't set down the cross-branches until you're ready to cook.

Pour in the beer and add the mustard, 1 teaspoon paprika, table salt, and ground pepper. Drizzle on the honey and top it all with the chiles and thyme. (You don't need to stir any of this.) Cover with the other skillet, inverted (no need for coals here), and cook until the chicken is cooked through and the sauce is thick and caramelized, about 25 minutes. Sprinkle with parsley before digging in.

CHICKEN FROM HELL

There's a reason we call this chicken from hell. It's fiery hot! For this, we like a mix of Thai green chiles and habaneros or Scotch bonnets, but use whatever fresh chiles you enjoy or have on hand. For the poppers, we use an orange jalapeño, but you may also use larger sweet mini peppers to tame the heat.

INGREDIENTS

6 jalapeño peppers

3½ ounces (100 g) fresh mozzarella cheese, sliced into small planks or sticks

1 small yellow onion, finely diced

5 fresh chiles, sliced (seeds retained for more heat)

4 garlic cloves, thinly sliced

2½ tablespoons (50 g) honey

1 lemon, thinly cut into 6 slices (reserve the remaining lemon)

1 (12-ounce, or 355 ml) bottle beer

3 chicken breasts, butterflied (do not cut all the way through)

Flaky sea salt

Freshly cracked black pepper

Sweet paprika for seasoning

1 to 2 tablespoons oil

Chopped fresh parsley for garnish

DIRECTIONS

Prepare your fire for medium heat.

Slice the jalapeños down one side, below the stem, taking care not to cut all the way through the peppers. Stuff each with mozzarella slices. Set aside.

In a small bowl, stir together the onion, fresh chiles, garlic, honey, juice from the remaining unsliced lemon, and beer.

Generously season the chicken on both sides with sea salt, cracked pepper, and paprika.

Place a large cast-iron skillet over medium heat and pour in the oil. When shimmering, add the chicken to the skillet. Cook until deeply golden brown and gorgeous, then flip. Cook for a couple minutes to sear, then add the beer mixture and bring it to a steady boil.

Nestle in the poppers, cheese-side up. Top the chicken with the lemon slices, then cover the skillet with an inverted skillet (or close the grill lid). Top with a large handful of coals, covering nearly the whole skillet, and cook until the chicken is done and the sauce is thickened, 20 to 25 minutes. You want this to cook slowly, so it's okay if the fire dies down as you replenish the coals on top.

Serve, sprinkled with parsley, along with the pan sauce and the poppers.

VEGETABLE-STUFFED CHICKEN BREAST

Chicken breast gets a bad rap for being bland and a bit boring. We kick up our version with a forest twist. Just imagine ratatouille stuffed into a chicken breast, drizzled with fresh pesto. Now, stop imagining it—and make it! We give approximate amounts of each veggie to use, but this isn't a science, and above all, we want you to have fun while you try something new. Don't worry if you cut too much or not enough—just go with it! Dip any extra veggies in the amazing pesto and enjoy it all with a cold beverage.

INGREDIENTS

For the chicken

3 or 4 chicken breasts

Olive oil

Flaky sea salt

Freshly cracked black pepper

½ (cut lengthwise) medium zucchini, sliced into thin half-moons (10 to 12 slices)

1 tomato, halved (vertically) and sliced into thin half-moons (10 to 12 slices)

½ onion, halved, then sliced (keeping the 10 to 12 slices intact)

1 (3½-ounce, or 100 g) block white cheddar cheese, cut into 8 to 10 planks

½ yellow bell pepper, cut vertically into 8 to 10 strips

1 (12-ounce, or 355 ml) bottle beer

Shredded mozzarella cheese for garnish

Chopped fresh parsley for garnish

For the pesto

1 cup (40 g) fresh basil leaves

6 tablespoons (50 g) pine nuts

4 garlic cloves, peeled

½ teaspoon table salt, plus more as needed

½ teaspoon ground black pepper, plus more as needed

6 tablespoons plus 2 teaspoon (100 ml) olive oil

Scant ⅓ cup (30 g) grated Parmesan cheese

Lemon wedges for squeezing

DIRECTIONS

Prepare your fire for medium heat.

To make the chicken

Slice into the top of the chicken, every ½ inch (1 cm) or so, taking care not to cut all the way through. Rub oil over the chicken and into all the cuts. Generously season the chicken on both sides with sea salt and cracked pepper.

Into the first cut, place one slice each of zucchini, tomato, and onion. It's easiest if you put the veggies together in a stack, then insert them as one.) Into the next cut, place a piece of cheese and bell pepper. (Again, stack them first, then insert them.) Repeat with the remaining zucchini, tomato, and onion and cheese and bell pepper, alternating stacks per cut on the chicken. Depending on the size of your chicken, you might end up with four tomato and three cheese, or an equal number of stacks—it doesn't matter!

continued

Place a large cast-iron skillet over medium heat and pour in 1 tablespoon (15 ml) oil. When shimmering, add the chicken to the skillet, then pour in the beer around it. Sprinkle the chicken with the mozzarella—just enough to add flavor, this isn't a pizza. Cover with an inverted skillet, place a handful of coals on top, and cook until the chicken is cooked through, there's good color on top, and the beer has mostly evaporated, about 20 minutes; replenish the coals as needed. Meanwhile, make the pesto.

To make the pesto

Use a mortar and pestle to pound the basil, pine nuts, garlic, table salt, and ground pepper into a paste. Pour in the oil and add the Parm and a squeeze of fresh lemon juice. Pound, or stir, until the desired consistency. (If you don't have a mortar and pestle, combine the ingredients in a food processor and pulse a few times, adding the oil last.) Taste for seasoning.

Serve the chicken with the pesto spooned over it and sprinkle with parsley before devouring.

BACON-WRAPPED CHICKEN POCKETS

We really like wrapping things in bacon. (Can you blame us?) For this recipe, use longer, thinner fresh chiles, rather than something squat like a habanero, and cut the sausage and cheese into planks about the length of the peppers. We also use a Polish seasoning called *przyprawa do kurczaka*. It comes in packets, similar to those for French onion soup mix or ranch dressing mix, and contains a mixture of chile and sweet peppers, mustard, ginger, marjoram, rosemary, and garlic. Depending on where you live, you can find it in grocery stores (we can get it at a Polish market here in Ireland) or online. Use whatever spice *you* like on chicken.

INGREDIENTS

For the chicken

3 chicken breasts

2 fresh chiles (red and/or green), halved lengthwise (seeds retained for more heat)

5⅓ ounces (150 g) sausage (such as smoked kielbasa), cut lengthwise into 3 planks

Scant 2 ounces (50 g) cheddar cheese, cut into 3 planks

18 bacon slices

1 to 2 tablespoons (15 to 30 ml) olive oil

About 11 ounces (300 g) baby potatoes (see 109)

2 or 3 thyme sprigs

2 or 3 rosemary sprigs

4 garlic cloves, peeled

3 tablespoons plus 1 teaspoon (50 g) butter

1 teaspoon table salt

1 teaspoon ground black pepper

1 teaspoon chicken spices (*przyprawa do kurczaka*)

1 (12-ounce, or 355 ml) bottle beer

Chopped fresh parsley for garnish

For the sauce

¼ yellow onion, finely chopped

3 garlic cloves, sliced

1 teaspoon table salt

½ teaspoon ground black pepper

3 tablespoons (45 g) plain yogurt

1 to 2 tablespoons (15 to 30 ml) olive oil

DIRECTIONS

Prepare your fire for medium heat.

To make the chicken

Cut a pocket into each chicken breast: use the tip of a sharp knife and start at the fatter end, taking care not to poke through the breast. Stuff a chile half, one piece of sausage, and one piece of cheese into the pocket. Chop the remaining chile half and reserve for the sauce.

On your cutting board, lay four bacon slices next to each other, vertically. In the middle of the strips, lay two bacon slices horizontally across the vertical strips, lining up the ends of the horizontal strips with the left edge of the vertical strips (so it looks like a sideways T).

Place a chicken breast on top of the horizontal bacon slices; it will cover all the way across the four vertical slices, and it's okay if the tail hangs off a bit. Pull the vertical slices at the bottom up and over the chicken, fold the two horizontal slices back and across the chicken, and, finally, pull the top vertical slices up and over the chicken. Repeat with the remaining bacon slices and chicken breasts.

continued

Place a large cast-iron skillet over medium heat and pour in the oil. When shimmering, add the potatoes. When they start to take on color, scoot them to one side of the skillet and add the chicken to the skillet, placing it on the side where the bacon ends fold over. Cook until the bacon starts to brown and the fat renders, 5 to 7 minutes, then flip the chicken. Flip the potatoes occasionally.

Add the thyme, rosemary, garlic, and butter to the skillet; sprinkle with salt, pepper, and chicken spices. Pour in the beer (it will bubble up). Cover with an inverted skillet (or close the grill lid) and place a large handful of coals on top, covering nearly the whole thing. Cook until the chicken and potatoes are cooked through and golden brown, about 20 minutes, replenishing the coals as needed. (When the beer evaporates, the chicken should be ready.)

To make the sauce

Using a mortar and pestle, mash the onion, garlic, reserved chile, salt, and pepper into a paste. Stir in the yogurt and 1 to 2 tablespoons (15 to 30 ml) oil. (If you don't have a mortar and pestle, combine the ingredients in a food processor and pulse a few times.) Spoon the sauce over the chicken and potatoes to serve and sprinkle with the parsley.

> To accompany this fancy chicken, we wanted fancy potatoes. We cut them like hasselback potatoes (see page 72) but in a cross-hatch pattern. It gets them nice and crispy, but feel free to stop at "hasselbacking" them.

TURKEY BREAST WITH CRANBERRY SAUCE

For this recipe, we prefer to use a Polish cheese called *oscypek*. It's a salted, smoked sheep's milk cheese made in the southern mountains of Poland, between late April and early October. Great for grilling—and particularly delicious with cranberry or lingonberry sauce—it's golden in color and has a decoration on it from the mold it's shaped in. We get it at a Polish market, but you can use any smoked cheese (mozzarella, Gouda) to achieve the same flavor.

INGREDIENTS

About 9 ounces (250 g) fresh cranberries

¾ cup plus 1 tablespoon plus 1 teaspoon (200 ml) fresh orange juice

3 tablespoons plus 1 teaspoon (50 g) brown sugar

2½ tablespoons (50 g) honey

2 star anise pods

2 cinnamon sticks

Grated zest of 1 orange

1 (1½-pound, or about 700 g) turkey breast, butterflied (do not cut all the way through)

Flaky sea salt

Freshly cracked black pepper

Handful of fresh baby spinach

5⅓ ounces (150 g) smoked cheese, about 1 ounce (30 g) grated, the rest cut into 4 pieces

1 tablespoon (15 ml) olive oil

¾ cup plus 1 tablespoon plus 1 teaspoon (200 ml) white wine

Chopped fresh parsley for garnish

DIRECTIONS

Prepare your fire for medium heat.

In a large cast-iron skillet over medium heat, combine the cranberries and orange juice and bring to a boil. Stir in the brown sugar, honey, star anise, cinnamon sticks, and orange zest. Simmer until the cranberries have broken down and the sauce is thick and jammy, 20 to 25 minutes.

Open the butterflied turkey breast like a book and season both sides with salt and pepper. With the breast cut-side up, spread three or four spoonfuls of the cranberry sauce over it and top with the spinach and grated cheese. Close the turkey breast (as if you're closing a book) and give it a couple pats to press everything together.

Place a grill pan over medium heat (see Forest Hack, page 98) and pour in the oil. When hot, add the turkey breast to the pan. Cook until deep golden grill marks form on both sides. Carefully add the wine—it will probably ignite on the open fire! (If you're using a gas grill, or this otherwise worries you, remove the pan from the flame before adding the wine, then return it to the heat.) Cover with an inverted skillet and top (or close the grill lid) and top with a large handful of coals to cover the whole skillet. Cook until the turkey breast is deep golden brown and cooked through, a good 25 to 30 minutes, replenishing the coals as needed.

Remove the turkey from the pan and add the cheese pieces. Cook until golden, with grill marks on both sides.

Slice the turkey (across the book) and spoon the remaining cranberry sauce over the top. Sprinkle with parsley and enjoy with the cheese.

FOREST HACK

Depending on the style of your grill pan (whether it has one handle or two), you might need the Two-Pan Holder on page 101 in addition to the Pan Stand on page 20. Have the bushcraft materials prepared before you start cooking, and when the cranberry sauce is done, simply switch out your setups. We do this all the time, and it really takes no time if everything's ready to be assembled.

DUCK BREASTS WITH SMASHED POTATOES

We had never cooked duck before, and we wanted to challenge ourselves to see what kind of recipe we could come up with. The result is one delicious dish. The key to cooking duck is to start it in a cold pan. If you try searing it on high heat, the fat will stay in the skin and not render, which means you'll not only have greasy duck, but you won't have any duck fat for finishing the potatoes. We've made the potatoes smashed, mainly because we don't see them called for very often, and they're extremely tasty when cooked over the fire.

INGREDIENTS

Table salt

About 1 pound, 2 ounces (500 g) baby potatoes (such as Yukon golds; about 6 potatoes)

2 duck breasts

Flaky sea salt

Freshly cracked black pepper

Ground black pepper

5 garlic cloves, peeled

4 thyme sprigs

2 rosemary sprigs

1 tablespoon (7.5 g) all-purpose flour

1 cup plus 2 teaspoons (250 ml) red wine

1 tablespoon (17.5 g) prepared cranberry sauce

7 ounces (200 g) fresh raspberries

½ cup plus 2 tablespoons (150 ml) chicken stock

2½ tablespoons (50 g) honey

Chopped fresh parsley for garnish

DIRECTIONS

Prepare your fire for high heat. (If using a grill, set up one side for high heat and one side for low/medium-low heat.)

Fill a large pot with 2 quarts (about 2 L) water, generously season the water with table salt, and bring it to a boil over high heat. Add the potatoes and boil just until tender on the outside and still a bit hard in the middle, about 15 minutes. Meanwhile, prep the remaining ingredients.

Prepare your fire for low (or medium-low) heat.

Score the skin of the duck breasts in a cross-hatch pattern and generously season both sides with sea salt and cracked pepper. Place the breasts, skin-side down, in a large cast-iron skillet and set it over low to medium-low heat. Cook until the fat renders and the skin is deeply golden brown. Flip the breasts and cook until the other side is golden. Flip the duck back onto the skin side and cover with an inverted skillet (or close the grill lid), placing coals on top; the skillet should be completely covered with coals, and there should be hardly any heat from beneath. It'll cook for 10 to 15 minutes total; duck is best served medium-rare (pinkish), but do as you like. Remove the duck from the skil-  let, leaving the beautiful, rendered duck fat behind, cover the duck to keep it warm, and build up the flame under the skillet again medium heat.

Drain the potatoes and place them on a cutting board. With the flat side of your knife, press into each potato to "smash," or flatten, it—do it carefully because you don't want to pulverize the potatoes. Transfer the potatoes to the skillet with the hot duck fat. Sprinkle with table salt and ground pepper and cook until golden brown. Flip the potatoes, add the garlic, thyme, and rosemary and cook until golden. Transfer the potatoes to the cutting board.

To the skillet, add the flour, stirring until cooked and no lumps remain, 1 to 2 minutes. Stir in the wine and cranberry sauce and cook until thickened. Add the raspberries, chicken stock, and honey. Boil until thick and jammy, 10 to 15 minutes.

Slice the duck breasts and spoon the sauce over them. Serve alongside the potatoes, sprinkled with parsley.

FOREST BAKING

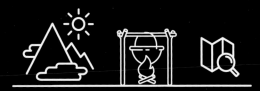

Hold on. Baking? *In the forest*? Although we admit these are probably our trickiest recipes to make, they are definitely the most rewarding. They're tricky because you shouldn't open your camp "oven" to peek at your dough, because doing so will cause the temperature inside to drop. (Our cook times are approximate because there's always that weather variable to contend with.) But when you have that first bite of a cheesy, saucy calzone or you dig in to Camembert baked in its own bread bowl, you'll understand why we keep baking in the forest. These recipes are so much more rewarding than when you simply turn on the oven in your kitchen!

SAUSAGE ROLLS

These sausage rolls would fit right in at a football tailgate, but we think their pretty presentation is enhanced by the great outdoors. The English mustard we call for is a hot yellow mustard, with a heat similar to that of horseradish or wasabi. It's most easily found under the Colman's brand. It might sound like we use a lot of it, but the mustard cuts through the fattiness of the sausage. It's a nice balance!

INGREDIENTS

For the dough

2½ cups (300 g) all-purpose flour

1 scant to heaping tablespoon (10 to 15 g) sugar

Scant 2 teaspoons active dry or instant yeast

1 teaspoon table salt

2 tablespoons plus 2 teaspoons (40 ml) melted butter (see Forest Hack, below)

¾ cup plus 1 tablespoon plus 1 teaspoon (200 ml) warm milk

For the mustard sauce

3 garlic cloves, peeled

1 fresh chile (seeds retained for more heat)

2 tablespoons (30 ml) olive oil

1 teaspoon table salt

1 teaspoon ground black pepper

6 tablespoons plus 2 teaspoons (100 g) plain yogurt

3 tablespoons (60 g) honey

2 tablespoons (30 g) English mustard or Dijon (but the flavor will be milder)

1 tablespoon (15 g) whole-grain mustard

1 tablespoon (6 g) grated lemon zest

Fresh parsley for garnish

For the filling

1 tablespoon plus 1 teaspoon (20 g) butter

1 tablespoon (15 ml) oil

1 yellow onion, finely chopped

4 garlic cloves, sliced

2 rosemary sprigs

About 14 ounces (400 g) pork sausage, casings removed

Heaping ½ cup (70 g) grated white cheddar cheese

Poppy seeds for garnish

Sesame seeds for garnish

Melted butter for brushing

DIRECTIONS

Prepare your fire for medium heat. (If using a grill, set up one side for medium heat and one side for low/indirect heat.)

To make the dough

In a large bowl, stir together the flour, sugar, yeast, and salt. Stir in the melted butter and about half the warm milk. Incorporate the flour, adding the remaining milk once the mixture gets too dry, until a shaggy dough ball forms. Knead until a smooth, pliable dough ball forms, 6 to 8 minutes. Cover with an inverted bowl and set the dough near the fire to rest while you prepare the other ingredients. See "Where's the Rise," on page 139.

> ## FOREST HACK
> Put your water and butter in camp cups and set them next to your fire while you gather your ingredients. They'll be warm enough (and melted) once you're ready to make your dough.

continued

To make the sauce

Use a mortar and pestle to pound the garlic and the chile until broken up. Add the oil, salt, and pepper and mix well. Stir in the yogurt, honey, English and whole-grain mustards, and lemon zest until well combined. Set aside. (If you don't have a mortar and pestle, combine the ingredients in a food processor and pulse a few times.)

To make the filling

In a large cast-iron skillet over medium heat, heat the butter and oil until the butter melts. Add the onion and garlic and cook until the vegetables start to soften and brown. Add the rosemary and cook until the onion is very soft and brown and the rosemary is a bit crispy. Transfer to a large bowl and, when cool enough to handle, strip the leaves from the rosemary.

To the bowl, add the sausage and cheese. Mix with your hands until everything is fully incorporated. Divide the sausage mixture into four equal portions and shape each portion into a log, 5 to 6 inches (13 to 15 cm) long.

Prepare your fire for low heat.

To assemble

Refer to the photo, page 117, to see what the finished plaited sausage rolls look like.

Divide the dough into four portions. Take one portion and roll it to about ⅛ inch (0.3 cm) thick (the length should be just a little bit longer than the sausage). Set a sausage log in the middle of the dough lengthwise. Starting at the log, on both sides, diagonally slash five or six cuts all the way to the edge of the dough. Then, starting at the top, fold one strip of dough over the log, pressing gently. Alternate with the top strip from the other side, and continuing down the log, alternately pressing each strip gently into the piece laid before it. Pinch the bottom edge closed. Repeat with the remaining dough and sausage logs.

Set the wrapped logs in a large well-seasoned cast-iron skillet and place it over smoldering coals or indirect heat. Brush with melted butter and sprinkle with poppy seeds and sesame seeds. Cover with an inverted skillet and place a large handful of coals on top—the lid should be nearly covered with hot coals, save for the very center (or close the grill lid). Cook until the sausage is cooked through and the dough is slightly puffed and very golden, about 40 minutes, replenishing the coals as needed.

Sprinkle the mustard sauce with parsley and use for dipping the sausage rolls.

FOREST HACK

With dough recipes, especially, we focus more on the heat from the top, to better simulate an oven. In fact, the fire beneath is nearly dead, and you might have only residual heat from the coals or ashes. In recipes such as this one, where we suggest covering nearly the whole inverted skillet with coals, keep the majority of coals on the edges of the skillet because the heat goes right into the middle. If you put the majority of your coals in the center of the "lid," the top of your bread will scorch.

SKILLET PIZZA

This pizza is, hands down, better than anything that can be delivered to your door. It even has a cheesy stuffed crust! You'll see we call for all-purpose flour in most of our yeast-dough recipes, including this one, and we mean it! If you're used to using bread flour with yeast, that's okay too, but we'd rather spend our time in the forest than hunting for specific flours. It'll be delicious either way—trust us. Top it however you like, but we stand by the smoked pork belly and chicken in a freshly made tomato sauce.

INGREDIENTS

For the pizza dough

2½ cups (300 g) all-purpose flour, plus more for dusting

1 tablespoon (18 g) table salt

Scant 2 teaspoons active dry or instant yeast

¾ cup plus 1 tablespoon plus 1 teaspoon (200 ml) warm water

2 tablespoons plus 2 teaspoons (40 ml) olive oil

For the sauce

1 tomato, finely chopped

½ small red onion, finely chopped

Scant ¼ cup (60 g) tomato paste

3 tablespoons plus 1 teaspoon (50 ml) olive oil

3 garlic cloves, minced

Large handful of fresh basil leaves, sliced

1 teaspoon dried oregano

1 teaspoon table salt

1 teaspoon ground black pepper

For the toppings

3½ ounces (100 g) smoked pork belly, cut into ½ × 1-inch (1 × 2.5 cm) pieces

1 chicken breast, cut into 1-inch (2.5 cm) pieces

1 teaspoon ground black pepper

1 teaspoon dried oregano

1 (7-ounce, or 200 g) block mozzarella cheese, cut into 6 "cheese sticks" (about the size of string cheese)

Scant ½ cup (50 g) shredded mozzarella cheese

1 fresh chile, thinly sliced (seeds retained for more heat)

½ small red onion, thinly sliced

Chopped fresh basil or parsley for garnish

DIRECTIONS

Prepare your fire for medium heat. (If using a grill, set up one side for medium heat and one side for low/indirect heat.)

To make the dough

In a large bowl, stir together the flour, salt, and yeast. Make a well in the center and pour in some of the warm water and the oil. Mix the dough until it gets dry, then add the remaining water, stirring until a wet, sticky dough forms. Sprinkle a bit of flour over the dough and knead until an elastic dough ball comes together, about 8 minutes. Drizzle with a little oil, cover with an inverted bowl, and set near the fire to rest while you prepare the remaining ingredients. See "Where's the Rise," on page 139.

continued

To make the sauce

In a medium bowl, stir together the tomato, onion, tomato paste, oil, garlic, basil, oregano, salt, and pepper until well mixed. Set aside.

To make the toppings

In a large cast-iron skillet over medium heat, cook the pork belly until it starts to brown and render its fat. Add the chicken and cook until browned on all sides. Stir in the pepper and oregano until evenly distributed. Remove the skillet from the heat.

Prepare your fire for low heat.

To assemble the pizza

Generously dust a cutting board with flour and set the pizza dough on it. (It might still be a bit sticky.) Sprinkle with more flour and give it a few good kneads. Stretch out the dough on the board, almost to the edge, using your fingertips to press and pull until the dough is about ½ inch (1 cm) thick all over. Place a ring of six mozzarella sticks around the edge of the dough, a good inch (2.5 cm) or so from the edge (see photo above). Fold the edges of the dough over the cheese sticks, tucking the dough under the cheese to seal it in. Transfer the crust to a large well-seasoned cast-iron skillet (it should fit snuggly) and place the skillet over low heat.

Spoon the sauce over the crust and sprinkle with the shredded cheese. Top with the cooked meats, chile slices, and onion. (You might not use all of the vegetables.) Cover with an inverted skillet and top with a large handful of coals (or close the grill lid). Cook until the crust is puffed and deeply brown on top, at least 25 minutes and up to 30, replenishing the coals as needed. Remove the pizza from the skillet and sprinkle with chopped basil before cutting and sharing.

FOREST HACK

Be very careful with these pizzas. We have burned many! Even though we call for low heat, there's actually almost no heat coming from the bottom—it's just enough heat to keep things going; use very thin sticks (the size of matchsticks) to keep the flame going.

FOREST PRETZELS

We take our pretzels seriously, which is why we take the time to put them in the traditional baking soda bath. This technique helps create a slightly crispier crust, a chewier interior, and that signature pretzel taste. Don't skip it! The zesty cheese sauce that accompanies these pretzels includes beer—use whatever brew you enjoy.

INGREDIENTS

For the pretzel dough

1¼ cups (300 ml) warm water

Scant 2 teaspoons active dry or instant yeast

1 tablespoon (15 g) brown sugar

1 teaspoon table salt

1 tablespoon plus 2 teaspoons (25 ml) melted butter (see Forest Hack)

3⅓ cups (400 g) all-purpose flour, plus more for dusting

2 tablespoons (27.6 g) baking soda

Sesame seeds for garnish

Poppy seeds for garnish

Coarse sea salt for garnish

For the cheese sauce

1 tablespoon plus 1 teaspoon (20 g) butter

¼ cup (30 g) all-purpose flour

6 tablespoons plus 2 teaspoons (100 ml) milk

1 (12-ounce, or 355 ml) bottle beer

1 teaspoon red pepper flakes, plus more as needed

1 teaspoon dried oregano, plus more as needed

1 teaspoon ground black pepper, plus more as needed

1 teaspoon garlic powder, plus more as needed

Scant 2 ounces (50 g) white cheddar cheese, grated

Scant 2 ounces (50 g) orange cheddar cheese, grated

Scant 2 ounces (50 g) blue cheese, crumbled

Chopped fresh parsley for garnish

DIRECTIONS

Prepare your fire for medium heat. (If using a grill, set up one side for medium heat and one side for low/indirect heat.)

To make the dough

In a large bowl, stir together the warm water and yeast until frothy. Stir in the brown sugar and table salt. Add the melted butter and stir to combine. Gradually add the flour, a bit at a time, stirring until it's all incorporated and a sticky dough forms. Dust a cutting board with flour and transfer the dough to it. Knead until a smooth yet pliable dough ball forms, 6 to 8 minutes. Cover with an inverted bowl and set near the fire while you make the cheese sauce. See "Where's the Rise," on page 139. (If you're using a grill, bring a pot of water to a simmer while you make the sauce.)

To make the cheese sauce

In a large cast-iron skillet over medium heat, melt the butter. Add the flour, stir until fully incorporated, and cook until it starts to turn color, 1 to 2 minutes. While stirring, stream in the milk and cook until very thick and almost paste-like. Add the beer and spices, stirring until well combined. When the mixture starts to bubble, add the cheeses and stir until completely melted, gooey, and amazing. Taste for seasoning and remove from the heat.

continued

HOW TO SHAPE PRETZELS LIKE A BAVARIAN

We don't judge, but pretzel shaping is easy. No doubt, your last pretzel will look better than your first!

1. Place the rope of dough in front of you horizontally.

2. Take the two ends and bring them up, forming a U.

3. Cross one end over the other by 2 inches (5 cm) or so. (Bavarians cross them over each other once more to form a little twist.)

4. Bring both ends down and over the bottom piece of dough (the original center of the rope).

5. Gently press where the ends cross over the bottom piece.

To finish

In a large pot over medium heat, combine 2 quarts (about 2 L) water and the baking soda and bring to a simmer.

Meanwhile, dust the cutting board with flour and place the dough on it. Cut the dough into three equal pieces. Roll each piece into a rope about the length of your board. Form each rope into a pretzel shape (see How to Shape Pretzels Like a Bavarian, above).

Gently transfer one pretzel at a time to the simmering water and boil for 45 seconds. Transfer the pretzel to the cutting board and sprinkle with a solid pinch each of sesame seeds, poppy seeds, and sea salt.

Prepare your fire for low heat.

Line a clean cast-iron skillet with parchment paper and set it over low heat. Arrange the pretzels in the skillet. Cover with an inverted skillet and place a handful of coals on top (or close the grill lid). Cook until the pretzels are cooked through and golden, 20 to 25 minutes, replenishing the coals as needed.

Serve the pretzels with the warm cheese sauce, sprinkled with chopped parsley.

FOREST HACK

Put your butter in a camp cup and set it next to your fire while you gather your ingredients. It'll be melted once you're ready to make your dough. While you're at it, put the water in a second cup to warm as well.

BAKED CAMEMBERT IN FOREST-MADE BREAD

If you're new to Camembert, get ready to love it. Made from cow's milk, this cheese is creamy and spreadable right out of the box (and it does come in a little wooden box). Once heated, Camembert oozes deliciousness. You can even eat the soft rind. If you can't find Camembert, look for a "baby" wheel of Brie, which is similar, but a little milder and a bit creamier.

DIRECTIONS

Prepare your fire for low heat (or low/indirect heat, if using a grill).

To make the dough

Mound the flour on a large cutting board and create a well in the middle. Add the yeast and salt. Pour in about half the warm water and gradually start stirring in flour from the mound, adding more water as you go. Pour in all but a couple tablespoons (about 30 ml) of the melted butter and knead until a smooth, stiff, yet pliable dough ball forms, 8 to 10 minutes. Cover with an inverted bowl and set by the fire to rest while you prepare the filling. See "Where's the Rise," on page 139.

continued

INGREDIENTS

For the bread dough

4 heaping cups (500 g) all-purpose flour

Scant 2 teaspoons active dry or instant yeast

1 teaspoon table salt

1¼ cups (300 ml) warm water

3 tablespoons plus 1 teaspoon (50 ml) melted butter, plus more for drizzling

For the filling

3 scant tablespoons (20 g) dried bread crumbs

Scant 2 ounces (50 g) chorizo sausage, finely diced

1 fresh chile, thinly sliced (seeds retained for more heat)

2 garlic cloves, thinly sliced

Handful of fresh basil leaves, sliced

2 rosemary sprigs, 1 left whole, the other torn into pieces

1 (about 9-ounce, or 250 g) wheel Camembert cheese

1 spring onion, sliced

To make the filling

Place the bread crumbs in a medium bowl and add the chorizo, chile, garlic, and basil. Toss to combine.

Place the dough ball in a large, well-seasoned cast-iron skillet and give it a few pats to flatten it just ever so slightly at the top. Use a sharp knife to score a cross-hatch pattern in the top. Drizzle generously with some of the remaining 2 tablespoons (30 ml) of melted butter and top with a whole rosemary sprig. Place the skillet over low heat or smoldering coals (or indirect heat) and cover with an inverted skillet (or close the grill lid). Top with a handful of coals—there should be more coals on top than flame beneath—and cook until the bread is nicely browned on top and cooked through, about 30 minutes, replenishing the coals as needed.

Remove the bread from the skillet and discard the rosemary. Cut a hole the size of your cheese wheel out of the top of the bread. Snack on the top as you position the cheese snugly into the hole. Cover the cheese with a couple smaller rosemary sprigs and a couple generous pinches of filling (you might not use it all). Drizzle with melted butter and return the bread to the skillet. Re-cover with an inverted skillet (or close the grill lid), top with coals, and cook until the top is deeply golden brown, 10 minutes tops. There should be lots of heat from the top and only residual heat from the bottom at this point.

Remove the bread from the skillet and cut it into quarters. Sprinkle with the spring onion before devouring.

FOREST HACK

Something we've learned along the way, particularly with bread recipes, is that the center of the skillet draws in all the heat from the top coals. As the bread rises, the top/center of the loaf tends to touch the top skillet, where it can start to scorch before the sides of the bread are done. When you put coals on the top skillet, leave the very center clear, and just mound the coals around the edges. We've also found that placing a small camp cup of water in the center of the top skillet helps keep the center cooler.

FLATBREAD WITH CARAMELIZED ONIONS AND GOAT CHEESE

Six onions might, at first, seem like a lot, but once they cook down, they make just enough to pile over these golden flatbreads. The onions really work well with the tangy goat cheese and peppery arugula. If you *do* end up with extra cooked onions, use them to top burgers, sausages, pasta, or even a salad.

INGREDIENTS

For the flatbread dough

2$\frac{1}{2}$ cups (300 g) all-purpose flour, plus more for dusting

1$\frac{1}{2}$ teaspoons baking powder

1 teaspoon sugar

1 teaspoon table salt

$\frac{3}{4}$ cup plus 1 tablespoon plus 1 teaspoon (200 ml) warm milk (see Forest Hack)

Small handful of fresh parsley, chopped

4 garlic cloves, chopped

Coarse sea salt

Olive oil for the pan

For the toppings

1 tablespoon (15 ml) oil

6 red onions, halved and thinly sliced

3 tablespoons plus 1 teaspoon (50 g) brown sugar

2 tablespoons plus 2 teaspoons (40 ml) balsamic vinegar

$\frac{1}{2}$ cup plus 2 tablespoons (150 ml) red wine

1 teaspoon table salt

1 teaspoon ground black pepper

5$\frac{1}{3}$ ounces (150 g) soft crumbled goat cheese

Handful of baby arugula

DIRECTIONS

Prepare your fire for medium heat. (If using a grill, set up one side for medium heat and one side for low/indirect heat.)

To make the dough

In a large bowl, stir together the flour, baking powder, sugar, and table salt. Create a well in the middle and pour in about half the warm milk. Stir to incorporate the flour, adding the rest of the milk as you go, until a shaggy dough ball forms (you might have to use your hands near the end). Knead until a smooth, pliable dough ball forms, 6 to 8 minutes. See "Where's the Rise," on page 139.

Lightly flour the cutting board. Cut the dough into four wedges. Use a rolling pin to roll one piece very thin, about the size of a large pita bread. Repeat with the remaining dough wedges, stacking them on top of one another off to the side of the board. Sprinkle some of the parsley, garlic, and sea salt on the board. Lay one of the rolled rounds on top of the seasonings and sprinkle with more parsley, garlic, and sea salt. Give it a few rolls with the pin to press all the flavorings into the dough. Repeat with the remaining seasonings and flatbreads.

Drizzle 2 to 3 teaspoons oil into a large cast-iron skillet over medium heat. Place a flatbread in the skillet and cook until lightly puffed and evenly golden on both sides (like a perfect pancake). Flip it a few times to make sure the inside is fully cooked and the toppings don't burn. Repeat with the remaining flatbreads, adding more oil to the skillet if necessary.

continued

This is a great recipe to remind us of the caveat: *always focus on one thing at a time*. Not only is it a nice way to be present in what you're doing, but it keeps you from burning stuff.

To make the toppings

Adjust your fire's heat a little bit, to medium-low, and return the skillet to the heat. Pour in the oil and heat until it's shimmering. Add the onions and cook until they start to brown. Add the brown sugar and vinegar and cook, stirring, for 1 minute. Stir in the wine, table salt, and pepper and let boil until the liquid is reduced and the onions are very soft and very dark in color, at least 20 minutes and up to 25. Check on the onions every few minutes and scrape up any stuck bits on the bottom of the skillet. (If it seems as if they're really sticking, or burning, add the smallest splash of water to loosen them up.) Remove the skillet from the heat. Transfer the onions to a bowl and carefully clean the skillet.

Prepare your fire for low heat.

Divide most of the goat cheese among the flatbreads. Top with the hot onions and a bit more cheese.

Return the clean skillet to the heat (indirect side, if using a grill) and place a flatbread in it. Cover with an inverted skillet and top with a full handful of coals (or close the grill lid). Cook until the cheese slightly softens and takes on a bit of golden color, about 5 minutes. Cook one flatbread at a time with the top skillet nearly covered in coals with very little heat from below. Top with a few leaves of arugula before cutting into halves or quarters.

CHEESE BREAD

This is one of the best breads we've ever eaten! We didn't plan on making it this way—it just looked nice all wrapped up, and it fit perfectly in the skillet. Bonus: because of all the butter, it forms a nice crust on the bottom. What more can you ask for?

INGREDIENTS

For the garlic butter

3 tablespoons plus 1 teaspoon (50 g) butter

4 garlic cloves, minced

Handful of fresh parsley, chopped

For the bread dough

3⅓ cups (400 g) all-purpose flour, plus more for dusting

1 tablespoon (12.5 g) sugar

1 tablespoon (18 g) table salt

Scant 2 teaspoons active dry or instant yeast

¾ cup plus 1 tablespoon plus 1 teaspoon (200 ml) water

3 tablespoons plus 1 teaspoon (50 ml) melted butter (see Forest Hack)

3 tablespoons plus 1 teaspoon (50 ml) buttermilk

For the filling

About 11 ounces (300 g) white cheddar cheese, grated

Chopped fresh parsley for garnish

Plain melted butter for the skillet

DIRECTIONS

Prepare your fire for low heat.

To make the garlic butter

Put the butter in a camp cup and set it near the fire to melt (or in a small saucepan on the grill). Stir in the garlic and parsley. Set aside.

To make the dough

In a large bowl, stir together the flour, sugar, salt, and yeast. Add the water and stir until the mixture becomes dry. Pour in the melted butter and stir to moisten the flour. Add the buttermilk and continue mixing until a shaggy dough ball forms (you might have to use your hands near the end). Knead until a smooth, pliable dough ball forms, 8 to 10 minutes. Set aside while you prepare the remaining ingredients. See "Where's the Rise," on page 139.

continued

To assemble

Generously flour a cutting board and place the dough on it. Use a rolling pin to roll the dough to about 11 × 18 inches (28 cm x 45 cm; we roll it right to the edges of our cutting board). Reserve a little bit of the garlic butter for brushing the top later and spoon the remaining garlic butter over the dough. Brush the butter until it's just about at the edge of the dough. Sprinkle the dough with the cheese.

Starting at one long end, loosely roll up the dough, setting the roll to rest on its seam. Give the ends a gentle pinch to seal. Now, starting at one end of the roll, with the roll still on its seam, curl the roll into itself. (It will resemble a snail shell.) The roll should not be tight, as it will expand when it cooks.

Brush the bottom and sides of a large cast-iron skillet over low heat with plain melted butter. Set the roll in the center of the skillet. Score the top a few times with a sharp knife and generously brush with the reserved garlic butter. Cover with an inverted skillet, top with a large handful of coals (or close the grill lid), and cook until the bread is puffed and deeply golden, about 30 minutes, replenishing the coals as needed. Remove the bread from the skillet and sprinkle with chopped parsley before cutting.

FOCACCIA WITH OIL AND VINEGAR DIP

On this beautiful focaccia, we decided to use pink salt, but as always, use whatever you like. This is one yeast dough for which we do recommend using bread flour as it results in a better texture. Lastly, we call for an approximate amount of olive oil because it's used throughout the recipe; our feeling is the more olive oil you use, the better the taste.

INGREDIENTS

For the focaccia

Heaping 4 cups (500 g) bread flour

Scant 2 teaspoons active dry or instant yeast

Pink salt

Scant 1½ cups (350 ml) warm water

About 3 tablespoons plus 1 teaspoon (50 ml) olive oil

⅔ cup (100 g) colorful cherry tomatoes, halved

1 (3½-ounce, or 100 g) block feta cheese, cubed (crumbled feta is okay, too)

½ small red onion, thinly sliced

Handful of green olives, halved

Chopped fresh parsley for garnish

For the bread dip

½ small red onion, diced

½ red bell pepper, diced

3 garlic cloves, peeled

1 teaspoon dried oregano

Generous pinch of pink salt

Generous pinch of freshly cracked black pepper

6 tablespoons plus 2 teaspoons (100 ml) olive oil

3 tablespoons plus 1 teaspoon (50 ml) balsamic vinegar

DIRECTIONS

Prepare your fire for low to medium-low heat.

To make the focaccia

In a large bowl, stir together the flour, yeast, and 1 teaspoon salt. Stir in the warm water, mixing until a shaggy dough ball forms (you might have to use your hands near the end). Knead until a smooth, pliable dough ball forms, 6 to 8 minutes.

Coat another clean large bowl with oil, place the dough in it, and invert the used bowl over it to cover. Set the dough near the fire to rest while you prepare the other ingredients (see Where's the Rise?, page 139).

Coat a large cast-iron skillet with oil and sprinkle it with salt. Invert the dough into the skillet (so the oiled side of the dough faces up) and use your fingertips to press it to the edges of the skillet. Cover with an inverted skillet and set aside to rest while you make the dip.

continued

To make the dip

Use a mortar and pestle to mash the onion, bell pepper, garlic, oregano, salt, and pepper into a smooth paste. Stir in the oil and vinegar, mixing well. (If you don't have a mortar and pestle, combine the ingredients in a food processor and pulse a few times.)

To finish

Use your fingertips to make dimples all over the bread. Top with the tomatoes, feta, onion, and olives. (You might not use all of the toppings—use as much as you like.) Drizzle with oil.

Set the skillet over low to medium-low heat and cover with an inverted skillet (or close the grill lid). Add a large handful of coals to the top, covering nearly the whole thing. Cook until the top of the bread is puffed and nicely golden, at least 25 minutes and up to 30, replenishing the coals as needed.

Transfer to a cutting board, cut the focaccia into wedges or blocks, sprinkle with parsley, and serve with the dip.

WHERE'S THE RISE?

If you've ever made a yeast dough before, you might be wondering why we don't allow our doughs to "rise until doubled in size," as most recipes state. For us, the weather plays a big role. We're very lucky if something doubles! Put simply, dough won't rise if it's cold outside, no matter how long we leave it, and if we put it near the fire too long, it will dry out. Rest assured that the short rests we recommend—while preparing the other ingredients—is enough. Just look at those photos if you need proof!

CALZONE

For these calzones, a friend recommended using salami—and it's what we now prefer to use. Use whatever *you* like, whether that's chorizo or pepperoni (or no meat at all). This recipe differs from some of the other baking recipes in that we use a higher heat from the bottom. The mozzarella has so much moisture, we had to raise the heat so there's no soggy crust. To even out the heat, we add more coals to the top.

INGREDIENTS

For the tomato sauce

4 tomatoes

2 tablespoons (30 ml) oil

1 small yellow onion, finely diced

3 garlic cloves, minced

1 teaspoon dried oregano

1 teaspoon table salt

1 teaspoon ground black pepper

Scant ¼ cup (60 g) tomato paste

2 tablespoons (40 g) honey

For the dough

Scant 3 cups (350 g) all-purpose flour, plus more for dusting

1 teaspoon table salt

1 cup minus 1 tablespoon (225 ml) warm water

Scant 2 teaspoons active dry or instant yeast

2 tablespoons (30 ml) olive oil, plus more for drizzling

For the filling

Handful of fresh basil leaves, chopped

About 2 ounces (60 g) salami, casing removed and diced

7 ounces (200 g) fresh mozzarella cheese, shredded

DIRECTIONS

Prepare your fire for low heat. (If using a grill, set up one side for medium heat and one side for low/indirect heat.)

To start the sauce
Score the tomatoes from top to bottom (cut as if you were quartering them, but only pierce the skin). Skewer the tomatoes (see Bushcraft, page 142) and hold them over a flame until the skins are charred and blistered. Peel and discard the skins and finely chop the tomatoes and set aside.

Prepare your fire for medium heat.

To make the dough
In a large bowl, stir together the flour and salt. In another bowl, stir together the warm water and yeast until foamy. Pour the yeast mixture into the flour and stir just until combined, then add the oil. Stir until a sticky dough ball comes together. Cover with an inverted bowl and set near the fire to rest while you prepare the sauce and filling.

To finish the sauce
In a large cast-iron skillet over medium heat, heat the oil. Add the onion and cook for a couple minutes, then add the garlic and cook for 1 minute. Add the chopped tomatoes, oregano, salt, and pepper and cook, stirring occasionally, until the tomatoes break down and the mixture thickens. Stir in the tomato paste and honey and cook for another minute or so until thick, glossy, and saucy. Remove from the heat.

continued

BUSHCRAFT
Make Your Own Campfire Spit

To blister the tomatoes for this recipe, you can certainly hold them over a fire like you would a marshmallow, but we need to keep our hands busy making the meal! Instead, we thread them on a spit and set them over the fire. Here's how:

1. Create the same setup as you would for the Noodle Drying Rack on page 28, knocking the posts on either side of the fire.

2. Choose a thin branch that's long enough to set between the forks and whittle it free of bark.

3. Whittle one end to a point and thread the point through the tomatoes.

To assemble

Generously dust a cutting board with flour and place the dough on it. Knead until a soft, pliable dough ball forms, 6 to 8 minutes. Halve the dough and set aside one half. Dust the remaining half with flour and pat it into a 9- or 10-inch (23 or 25 cm) circle, give or take. Spread 2 generous spoonfuls of sauce around the middle of the dough, leaving a good inch (2.5 cm) around the edge uncovered. Sprinkle half the sauce with half the basil, half the salami, and half the cheese. Pull one side of the dough (the side without the basil, etc.) over the filling and bring it to the other side, forming a half-moon shape. Crimp and pleat the edges to seal. Repeat with the remaining dough, sauce, and filling.

Transfer both calzones to a large well-seasoned cast-iron skillet over medium heat. Cover with an inverted skillet (or close the grill lid), and place an extra-large handful of coals on top. Cook until the crust is deeply browned, 20 to 25 minutes, replenishing the coals as needed. Set the calzones aside to cool, if desired (see Bushcraft, at right), before devouring.

BUSHCRAFT
Make Your Own Cooling Rack

There's nothing that says you can't eat these calzones right out of the skillet, but that filling is screaming hot! If you'd like to set them aside to cool for a bit (and you need something to do while they're cooking), you might make a cooling rack for them. Here's how:

1. Create the same setup as you did for the Campfire Spit (see previous page), times two, or make the Two-Pan Holder on page 101.

2. Place the two setups off to the side, not around the fire, about 1 foot (30 cm) apart.

3. Whittle several young green branches and set them between the two cross-branches.

CAMPFIRE DOUGHNUTS

These doughnuts are made in the traditional way—that is, they're deep-fried. True, that's not the same as baking, but you *could* bake the doughnuts, which is why they're in this chapter. But forget about all that triviality and focus instead on the accompanying sauces that will blow your tastebuds. There's a luscious mixed berry sauce and a silky chocolate whisky sauce—you won't be able to choose between them, so be sure to make (and eat!) both.

INGREDIENTS

For the dough

Scant 3 cups (350 g) all-purpose flour

3 heaping tablespoons (40 g) granulated sugar

1½ teaspoons baking powder

1 teaspoon table salt

1 cup plus 2 teaspoons (250 ml) buttermilk

3 tablespoons plus 1 teaspoon (50 ml) melted butter (see Forest Hack)

2 quarts (about 2 L) oil

For the mixed berry sauce

1 tablespoon plus 2 teaspoons (25 g) butter

7 ounces (200 g) fresh strawberries, hulled and finely chopped

3½ ounces (100 g) fresh blackberries

2 tablespoons (40 g) honey

For the chocolate whisky sauce

1 tablespoon plus 2 teaspoons (25 g) butter

7 ounces (200 g) chocolate (a mixture of dark and milk), chopped

1½ cups (300 ml) whisky

Grated zest of 1 lemon

Grated zest of 1 lime

For decoration

2 tablespoons (15 g) confectioners' sugar

Chopped fresh mint for garnish

DIRECTIONS

Prepare your fire for medium heat.

To make the dough

In a large bowl, stir together the flour, sugar, baking powder, and salt. In a smaller bowl, combine the buttermilk and melted butter. Pour the buttermilk into the flour mixture and mix well. Knead until a soft, smooth dough ball forms. Tear off pieces of dough (somewhere between the size of a golf ball and a tennis ball) and roll between your palms to form balls. Cover with a bowl and set aside while you prepare the sauces.

To make the mixed berry sauce

In a large cast-iron skillet over medium heat, melt the butter. Stir in the strawberries and cook for a couple minutes. Add the blackberries and cook, stirring occasionally, until the fruit is completely broken down and jammy. Stir in the honey and bring the sauce to a boil. All told, the sauce will take 10 to 15 minutes to cook. Transfer to a bowl and carefully clean the skillet.

continued

FOREST HACK

Put your butter in a camp cup and set it next to your fire while you gather your ingredients. It'll be melted by the time you're ready to make your dough.

To make the chocolate whisky sauce

Return the clean skillet to medium heat and add the butter to melt. Add the chocolate and cook, stirring constantly, until the chocolate is melted and smooth. Carefully pour in the whisky—it will ignite! (If you're using a gas grill, or this otherwise worries you, remove the pan from the flame before adding the whisky, then return it to the heat.) Let it burn; it will continue to burn while it thickens, but don't let it go too long. You don't want to burn off all the alcohol—you want to taste the whisky. The sauce won't take more than 10 minutes to make. Stir in the lemon zest and lime zest to taste and transfer the sauce to a bowl.

To make the doughnuts

Prepare your fire for medium-high heat.

Set a large pot over the heat and carefully pour in the oil. When hot (see Forest Hack, at right), carefully add a few doughnuts and cook until they're deeply golden and they float, 4 to 6 minutes. Cook the doughnuts in batches; do not crowd the pot. Use tongs, a spider, or a slotted spoon to remove the cooked doughnuts from the oil and transfer to a serving board. Repeat with the remaining doughnuts. Sprinkle the cooked doughnuts with confectioners' sugar and mint while warm and serve with the sauces for dipping.

FOREST HACK

The optimal oil temperature for deep-frying is between 350°F and 375°F (180°C and 190°C). To test whether the oil is hot enough, dip the handle of a wooden spoon or whittled stick into it. If there are steady bubbles in the oil, it's ready. Super vigorous bubbles—too hot. Few bubbles—too cold.

FROM THE SEA AND INTO THE FOREST

Being on social media, we often field cheeky questions (in addition to all the positive vibes). When we first posted a fish video, someone asked, "Where do you get fish in the forest?" as if to say it's absurd. Naturally, we get our fish in the same place as our other ingredients! It's not like we can get a lamb chop or chicken leg from the forest, either, so don't let the idea of seafood intimidate you. Although fish does cook quickly, we, of course, want to up the ante a bit and make the recipes more enticing. We wrap our salmon in pastry, beer-batter our fish to deep-fry with chips, and simmer a curry so fragrant we swear the whole forest smelled of it. You owe it to yourself to give these recipes a shot.

PASTRY-WRAPPED SALMON

You *could* call this recipe "Salmon Wellington with Hollandaise, Forest Edition" because that's basically what it is: fresh salmon topped in a sweet and spicy spinach mixture and wrapped in delicate pastry you make yourself. Drizzled with an elegant lemony sauce, it's a meal fit for a King (or Queen) of the Forest!

INGREDIENTS

For the salmon

6 tablespoons plus 2 teaspoons (100 g) butter, divided

2½ cups (300 g) all-purpose flour

Scant 2 teaspoons active dry or instant yeast

1 teaspoon sugar

Table salt

½ cup plus 2 tablespoons (150 ml) milk

2 tablespoons (30 ml) oil

4 garlic cloves, sliced

2 fresh chiles, chopped (seeds retained for more heat)

2½ tablespoons (50 g) honey

Juice of ½ lime

Large handful of fresh baby spinach

Scant ¼ cup (60 g) ricotta

1 (8½- to about 11-ounce, or 240 to 300 g) salmon fillet, skin removed

Ground black pepper

1 large egg yolk, beaten

For the sauce

3 large egg yolks

Juice of ½ lemon

Pinch of table salt

Pinch of ground black pepper

6 tablespoons plus 2 teaspoons (100 ml) melted butter

Chopped fresh parsley for garnish

DIRECTIONS

Prepare your fire for low heat.

To make the salmon

Put 5 tablespoons plus 1 teaspoon (80 g) of butter in a camp cup and set it near the fire to melt. (Or put it in a small saucepan and place it on the grill.)

In a large bowl, stir together the flour, yeast, sugar, and 1 teaspoon salt. Add the milk and melted butter from the camp cup, stirring until a rough dough comes together (you'll have to use your hands near the end). Knead until a smooth, pliable dough ball forms, 6 to 8 minutes. Cover the dough with another bowl and place it near the fire to rest while you prepare the other ingredients.

Pour the oil into a large cast-iron skillet over low heat and add the remaining 1 tablespoon plus 1 teaspoon (20 g) butter to melt. Add the garlic and chiles and cook until softened. Stir in the honey and lime juice. Add the spinach, enough to fill your skillet, and cook until the spinach is wilted and blended into the sauce. Stir in the ricotta until well blended throughout. Remove the skillet from the heat.

Generously dust a cutting board with flour and place the dough on it. Give the dough a few kneads. Halve the dough and reserve one half for another use. With a rolling pin, roll the remaining dough half to about the size of your board (ours is 11 × 18 inches, or 28 cm x 45 cm).

continued

Place a piece of salmon in the center of the dough and sea-son it with salt and pepper. Top the salmon with a spoonful or two of the spinach mixture to cover. Spread the egg yolk along the bottom (long) edge of the dough and along the two sides—it doesn't need to go all the way to the edge on the sides, just the inch (2.5 cm) or so nearest the salmon. Fold the top of the dough down and over the salmon, pressing it gently into the fish. Fold up the bottom piece so the egg yolk portion rests over the first piece of dough, pressing it together gently. Press down along both sides of the salmon, sealing the edges where the egg yolk is. Cut off all but about 1 inch (2.5 cm) of dough from either side and use the tines of a fork to press and seal the edges. Gently press the fork along the top seam, too.

Place the parcel in a large well-seasoned cast-iron skillet over low heat. Brush the top with egg yolk, sprinkle with salt, and cover with an inverted skillet (or close the grill lid). Set a large handful of coals on top, covering nearly the whole thing, and cook until the top of the pastry is nice and golden brown, 15 to 20 minutes, replenishing the coals as needed. Remove from the skillet to cool while you make the sauce.

To make the sauce
In a small bowl, combine the egg yolks, lemon juice, salt, and pepper. While stirring (or whisking), slowly pour in the melted butter until the sauce is creamy and emulsified. (The hot butter slowly cooks the yolks.)

Cut the salmon parcel in half, drizzle with the sauce, and sprinkle with parsley to serve.

FOREST FISH CAKES

Fish cakes are often leftover-dinner fare, making creative use of yesterday's cooked fish. But they needn't be! These crispy golden cakes are packed with aromatic veggies and served with a lemony sauce that certainly earns them a spot on the "What's for Dinner?" menu. We use cod here, which is a great choice for fish cakes because it's inexpensive and easy to cook (especially in the forest). Haddock makes a good substitute, as does halibut or any other flaky white fish.

INGREDIENTS

For the fish cakes

Table salt

4 medium potatoes, peeled and chopped

1 tablespoon plus 2 teaspoons (25 g) butter

6 tablespoons plus 2 teaspoons (100 ml) milk

About 11 ounces (about 600 g) skinless cod, cut into 4 fillets (to fit the pan)

1 small red onion, finely diced

1 spring onion, sliced

4 garlic cloves, sliced

1 fresh red chile, finely diced (seeds retained for more heat)

1 teaspoon whole-grain mustard

1 teaspoon ground black pepper

Grated zest of 1 lemon

¾ cup plus 1 heaping tablespoon (100 g) all-purpose flour

2 or 3 large eggs, beaten

1⅓ cups (150 g) bread crumbs

Oil for frying

For the sauce

3 tablespoons plus 1 teaspoon (50 ml) olive oil

Juice of ½ to 1 lemon, plus more as needed

½ teaspoon table salt, plus more as needed

½ teaspoon ground black pepper, plus more as needed

Small handful of fresh parsley leaves, coarsely chopped, plus more for garnish

DIRECTIONS

Prepare your fire for high heat. (If using a grill, set up one side for high heat and one side for medium heat.)

To make the fish cakes

Fill a large pot with 2 quarts (about 2 L) water, generously season the water with salt, and bring it to a boil over high heat. Add the potatoes and boil until tender and easily pierced with a skewer, 15 to 20 minutes. Meanwhile, prep the remaining ingredients.

Prepare your fire for medium heat.

In a large cast-iron skillet over medium heat, combine the butter and milk. When the butter melts, stir to combine, then add the cod. Simmer until the fish is cooked through and flakes easily, about 10 minutes.

Drain the potatoes and place them in a medium bowl. Add the red onion, spring onion, garlic, chile, mustard, 1 teaspoon salt, pepper, and lemon zest. Mash to combine. Flake in the fish and mash to form a thick paste, like very thick mashed potatoes. Form the mixture into patties, about 2 inches (5 cm) across and ½ inch (1 cm) thick (you'll get eight to ten cakes).

continued

Set up a breading station with the flour in one bowl (or mounded on your cutting board), the eggs in another bowl, and the bread crumbs in another. Coat each fish cake in the flour, then dip in the egg, allowing the excess egg to drip off, then coat in the bread crumbs, making sure to coat the edges, too.

Clean the skillet, place it over medium heat, and pour in enough oil to coat the bottom. When shimmering, add the fish cakes. (Do this in batches, if they don't all fit.) Cook until golden brown and crispy on both sides, 3 to 4 minutes per side. Meanwhile, make the sauce.

To make the sauce
In a small bowl, stir together the oil, lemon juice, salt, pepper, and parsley. Taste for seasoning, then drizzle the sauce over the cakes. Sprinkle with more parsley before noshing.

FISH CURRY

Although we've had chicken curry plenty of times, we'd never eaten fish curry. We thought fish curry *in the forest* would be something new. To that end, choose any white fish you like—barramundi, haddock, halibut, pollock, even salmon can stand up to these flavors, and this heat.

INGREDIENTS

1 cup (200 g) short-grain white rice

Table salt

2 tablespoons (30 ml) oil

1 red onion, finely diced

4 garlic cloves, thinly sliced

1- to 2-inch (2.5 to 5 cm) piece fresh ginger, peeled and finely chopped

2 tomatoes, 1 diced, 1 quartered

3 tablespoons (19 g) curry powder

1 tablespoon (5.6 g) red pepper flakes

1 tablespoon (7 g) ground cumin

1 tablespoon (6.8 g) ground turmeric

¾ cup plus 1 tablespoon plus 1 teaspoon (200 ml) vegetable stock

2 tablespoons (32 g) tomato paste

3 fresh chiles, sliced (seeds retained for more heat)

2 bell peppers, any color, cut into strips

1 cup plus 2 teaspoons (250 ml) coconut milk

About 11 ounces (300 g) cod fillets, cut into 2-inch (5 cm) chunks

Lime wedges for seasoning

Chopped fresh parsley or cilantro for garnish

DIRECTIONS

Prepare your fire for medium heat.

In a large cast-iron pot, combine the rice and a good pinch of salt. Pour in enough water to cover the rice by ¾ inch (1.5 cm). Cover the pot with a tight-fitting lid and place it over medium heat. Cook until the water is absorbed, 15 to 20 minutes. Meanwhile, prepare the remaining ingredients.

In a large cast-iron skillet over medium heat, heat the oil until shimmering. Add the onion, garlic, and ginger. Cook until softened and caramelized. Stir in the diced tomato, spices, and 1 teaspoon salt. Cook until the tomato is broken down, just a few minutes, then pour in the stock and stir in the tomato paste. Bring the mixture to a boil and add the chiles, bell peppers, and quartered tomato. Cook until the tomato and peppers are softened, a few minutes, then add the coconut milk, stirring until well blended. Add the fish and simmer until cooked through, 5 to 7 minutes.

Spoon the curry over the rice. Squeeze over a wedge of lime and add a sprinkle of fresh parsley.

COD WRAPPED IN BACON

We've said it before: everything tastes better with bacon, and cod is no exception. The fresh chopped salad on the side cuts through the richness and smokiness of that bacon, but use as much (or as little) of the salad ingredients as you like to round out your meal.

DIRECTIONS

Prepare your fire for medium heat.

In a large bowl, combine the cucumber, onion, tomato, bell pepper, and pineapple. Drizzle with just enough oil to coat, but not pool, and toss to combine. Season with salt, pepper, and fresh parsley to taste. Taste for seasoning and set aside.

On a cutting board, lay down five bacon slices, just slightly overlapping each other. In the middle of these, place two bacon slices perpendicular to them. Lay two more perpendicular slices, going the other way, so you have a cross. Place a piece of fish in the middle (at the narrow ends on the two bacon slices), and generously season with salt, pepper, and dried parsley.

Wrap two bacon slices over the top of the fish, then do the same with the other two slices. Alternate wrapping the five bacon slices from either side. Repeat with the remaining fish, bacon, and spices.

Place a grill pan over medium heat and drizzle in 1 to 2 tablespoons (15 to 30 ml) of oil. Place the fish in the pan, bacon-ends-side down. Cook until golden brown and sizzling, then flip. Get a nice color to the bacon before adding the wine to the skillet. Continue cooking until the wine evaporates and the fish is cooked through, 10 to 15 minutes.

Slice the fish and spoon the salad over it and add a lemon wedge for squeezing.

INGREDIENTS

½ to 1 English cucumber, peeled and diced

1 small red onion, finely diced

1 tomato, diced

1 yellow bell pepper, diced

½ pineapple, peeled, cored, and diced (see page 88)

Olive oil

Table salt

Ground black pepper

Chopped fresh parsley for seasoning

Bacon slices (about 22 slices)

2 (7-ounce, or 200 g) skinless cod fillets

Dried parsley for garnish

¾ cup plus 1 tablespoon plus 1 teaspoon (200 ml) white wine

Lemon wedges for seasoning

DRUNK SALMON

There are plenty of "drunk" recipes out there, but we have to admit that, even we were surprised at how well the flavors of salmon and whisky go together; this dish will blow your mind (and your taste buds!). When paired with a whisky-mustard vinaigrette on the simple chopped salad, this meal is next level.

INGREDIENTS

1 romaine lettuce heart, chopped (use any lettuce you like)

½ to 1 English cucumber, peeled and chopped

1 tomato, chopped

½ yellow or red onion, finely diced

7 ounces (200 g) feta cheese, cubed or crumbled

1 to 2 tablespoons (15 to 30 ml) whisky, plus ¾ cup plus 1 tablespoon plus 1 teaspoon (200 ml)

2 tablespoons (30 ml) olive oil, plus more for the fish

2½ tablespoons (50 g) honey

2 tablespoons (30 g) whole-grain mustard

Juice of ½ lemon, plus 9 lemon slices

Table salt

Ground black pepper

Small handful of fresh parsley, coarsely chopped, plus more for garnish

1 (about 11-ounce, or 300 g) skin-on piece of salmon

DIRECTIONS

Prepare your fire for medium heat.

In a large bowl, toss together the lettuce, cucumber, tomato, onion, and feta.

In a medium bowl, stir together 1 to 2 tablespoons (15 to 30 ml) whisky, oil, honey, mustard, lemon juice, ½ teaspoon salt, ½ teaspoon pepper, and parsley. Pour some of the dressing over the salad (just enough to moisten, not pool) and gently toss to coat and combine. Taste for seasoning and set aside.

Place a grill pan over medium heat. Drizzle the fish with oil, generously season with salt and pepper, and place it in the pan, skin-side down. Cook until the skin is nice and brown. Remove from the pan and, in its place, lay the lemon slices, slightly overlapping to form a bed for the fish. Return the salmon to the pan, setting it skin-side up on the lemon. Cook for a couple minutes, then carefully pour in the remaining ¾ cup plus 1 tablespoon plus 1 teaspoon (200 ml) whisky—it will likely ignite! (If you're using a gas grill, or this otherwise worries you, remove the pan from the flame before adding the whisky, then return it to the heat.)

Let the whisky burn off until the pan is nearly dry and the salmon is cooked through, 10 to 15 minutes.

Serve with the salad, pouring any remaining vinaigrette over the top and sprinkling with more parsley.

DELICIOUS PRAWN PASTA

Although we call this recipe "prawn pasta," what we're really after are shrimp, which we call "prawns" in the U.K. (Plus, the alliteration is nice.) Prawn and shrimp are actually two different crustaceans; shrimp are a bit smaller and tend to be easier to find in grocery stores—at least in the United States. Prawns are a bit meatier and, some say, a little sweeter, and they'd be a terrific addition to this dish if you can find them.

INGREDIENTS

Table salt

For the noodles

2½ cups (300 g) bread flour

1 teaspoon table salt

½ cup plus 2 tablespoons (150 ml; more or less) warm water (see Forest Hack, page 164)

For the prawns/shrimp

2 tablespoons (30 g) butter

2 tablespoons (30 ml) olive oil

1 small yellow onion, finely chopped

4 garlic cloves, sliced

1-inch (2.5 cm) piece fresh ginger, peeled and finely chopped

2 bell peppers, any color, cut into strips

2 fresh chiles (red and/or green), sliced (seeds retained for more heat)

3½ ounces (100 g) broccoli florets

¾ cup plus 1 tablespoon plus 1 teaspoon (200 ml) white wine

2 tablespoons (30 ml) soy sauce

1 teaspoon red pepper flakes, plus more as needed

1 teaspoon ground black pepper, plus more as needed

Scant 9 ounces (250 g) peeled and deveined shrimp (small or medium work best)

1 spring onion, sliced

DIRECTIONS

Prepare your fire for high heat. (If using a grill, set up one side for high heat and one side for medium heat.)

Fill a large pot with 2 quarts (about 2 L) water, generously season the water with salt, and bring it to a boil over high heat.

To make the dough

Mound the flour on a large cutting board and create a well in the middle. Sprinkle with the salt and add the warm water, gradually stirring in flour from the mound and adding more water as needed until all the flour is fully incorporated (you might have to use your hands near the end). Knead until a smooth, pliable dough ball forms, about 8 minutes.

Generously flour the board and dough. Use a rolling pin to roll the dough very thin, about 1/16 inch (0.16 cm) thick—about the height of your board (ours is 11 × 18 inches, or 28 cm x 45 cm). Cut the dough into strips, about ¼ inch (0.6 cm) wide (see Forest Hack, page 164). Sprinkle with flour and gently toss to loosen the noodles.

continued

FOREST HACKS

Put your water in a camp cup and set it next to your fire while you gather your ingredients. It'll be warm enough once you're ready to make your dough.

Here's an easy way to cut noodles evenly: Pick up either the top or bottom edge of the well-floured dough and fold it on itself, accordion style, folding back and forth four times, for a total of five layers. It will look like a neatly folded letter, the width of your board. To form the noodles, simply cut across the pleats every ¼ inch (0.6 cm) or so.

Add the noodles to the boiling water. Stir to separate and boil just until cooked through, about 90 seconds. Drain, reserving a bit of the cooking water. Place the noodles in a bowl with a bit of cool water mixed with a bit of the cooking water, just enough to coat but not submerge the noodles.

Prepare your fire for medium heat.

To make the prawns/shrimp

In a large cast-iron skillet over medium heat, combine the butter and oil. When the butter melts and the oil is shimmering, add the onion, garlic, and ginger and cook until fragrant. Add the bell peppers and chiles and cook until they just start to soften, then add the broccoli and cook until it is bright green. Stir in the wine, soy sauce, red pepper flakes, and black pepper. Taste for seasoning.

Add the shrimp, toss to coat, and cover with an inverted skillet (no need for coals here; or close the grill lid). Cook until the shrimp are opaque and curled, not more than 5 minutes, then add the noodles. Toss to coat, sprinkle with the spring onion, and serve.

CREAMY SALMON PASTA

You can thank Krzys for this recipe. He likes fish, so that's why we did it! It's also a relatively quick recipe to make, even with making the noodles. Plus, it's really delicious.

INGREDIENTS

Table salt

For the pasta

1⅔ cups (200 g) all-purpose flour, plus more for dusting

2 large eggs

3 large egg yolks

1 tablespoon (15 ml) olive oil (optional)

Pinch of table salt

For the salmon

Olive oil

About 11 ounces (300 g) skin-on salmon fillet

1 lemon, cut into wedges

Table salt

Ground black pepper

2 thyme sprigs

2 rosemary sprigs

3 garlic cloves, peeled

For the sauce

2 tablespoons (30 g) butter

4 garlic cloves, sliced

¾ cup plus 1 tablespoon plus 1 teaspoon (200 ml) heavy cream

2 tablespoons plus 2 teaspoons to ¼ cup (40 to 60 ml) white wine

Grated zest of 1 lemon

1 teaspoon table salt

1 teaspoon ground black pepper

Handful of fresh baby spinach

Chopped fresh parsley for garnish

DIRECTIONS

Prepare your fire for high heat. (If using a grill, set up one side for high heat and one side for medium heat.)

Fill a large pot with 2 quarts (about 2 L) water, generously season the water with salt, and bring it to a boil over high heat.

To make the pasta

Mound the flour on a large cutting board and create a well in the middle. Crack the eggs and into the well and add the yolks, drizzle in the oil (if using), and sprinkle with the salt. Using a fork, break up the eggs and gradually start stirring in flour from the mound until all the flour is fully incorporated and you have a dry, craggy-looking dough ball (you might have to use your hands near the end). Knead until a smooth, stiff, yet pliable dough ball forms, 8 to 10 minutes.

Generously flour the board and place the dough on it. Halve the dough, setting aside one half for another use. Use a rolling pin to roll the remaining dough very thin, about ¹⁄₁₆ inch (0.16 cm) thick—nearly the size of your board (ours is 11 × 18 inches, or 28 × 45 cm). Cut the dough into strips, about ¼ inch (0.6 cm) wide (see Forest Hack, page 166). Sprinkle with flour and gently toss to loosen the noodles. Hang the noodles over a drying rack (see page 28) or the back of a clean chair to dry while you prep the remaining ingredients and the water comes to boil. (Touching is okay, but try not to overlap or clump the noodles.)

continued

BUSHCRAFT
Make Your Own Rolling Pin

What's that? You forgot to pack your rolling pin? No problem. You can very easily make a straight-style pin (that is, without handles). Here's how:

1. Find a straight branch, 12 to 18 inches (30 to 45 m) long and about 2 inches (5 cm) in diameter.

2. Whittle off the bark. (It doesn't have to be perfect!)

3. Hold it over the fire for a few seconds to seal and remove any errant shavings.

Add the noodles to the boiling water. Stir to separate the noodles and boil just until cooked through, about 90 seconds. Drain, reserving a bit of the cooking water. Place the noodles in a bowl with a bit of cool water mixed with a bit of the cooking water, just enough to coat but not submerge the noodles.

Prepare your fire for medium heat.

To make the salmon
Drizzle some oil into a large cast-iron skillet and place it over medium heat. Add the salmon, skin-side down. Squeeze some lemon juice over the fish and season well with salt and pepper. Add the thyme, rosemary, and whole garlic to the skillet. Cook the fish on both sides until done to your liking, 10 to 12 minutes total, adding more lemon juice, salt, and pepper after flipping it. Transfer the fish to a plate and clean the skillet.

To make the sauce
Return the clean skillet to medium heat and add the butter to melt. Add the sliced garlic, cream, and wine. Cook until the mixture starts to bubble, then stir in the lemon zest, salt, pepper, and spinach. Cook until the spinach is wilted, add the pasta, and toss to coat.

Serve the salmon with the pasta and lemon wedges, sprinkled with parsley.

FOREST HACK

Here's an easy way to cut noodles evenly: Pick up either the top or bottom edge of the well-floured dough and fold it on itself, accordion style, folding back and forth four times, for a total of five layers. It will look like a neatly folded letter, the width of your board. To form the noodles, simply cut across the pleats every ¼ inch (0.6 cm) or so.

FISH AND CHIPS WITH MUSHY PEAS

Fish and chips may be standard British pub fare, but you won't taste anything better in a tavern than what you can make yourself out in the forest. We even have the mushy peas to maximize the experience! (If you're not a fan of mushy peas and prefer a side of coleslaw, head over to page 96.) We add a special twist to our beer-battered fish by adding kale to the mix, which not only looks nice, but gets good and crispy in the oil. The recipe looks like a lot of moving parts, but it's really not a lot of work when you have all day in the forest.

INGREDIENTS

For the potatoes
4 potatoes, cut into chips/fries (russets or Maris Pipers are great for this)

1 gallon (about 4 L) oil

For the tartar sauce
2 Polish dill pickles, finely chopped

½ shallot, finely diced

4 garlic cloves, sliced

3 tablespoons (45 g) plain yogurt

2 tablespoons (30 g) mayonnaise

1 tablespoon (15 g) whole-grain mustard

Juice of ½ lemon, plus more as needed

1 teaspoon table salt, plus more as needed

1 teaspoon ground black pepper, plus more as needed

Handful of fresh parsley, coarsely chopped

For the "mushy peas"
1 tablespoon (15 ml) oil

3 tablespoons plus 1 teaspoon (50 g) butter

⅔ cup (100 g) fresh peas

Table salt

Ground black pepper

1 tablespoon (15 g) whole-grain mustard

For the fish
1¼ cups (150 g) self-rising flour (see page 170)

2 heaping cups (500 ml) beer

Handful of fresh kale leaves, coarsely chopped

1 tablespoon (5.6 g) red pepper flakes

1 teaspoon table salt

1 teaspoon ground black pepper

1 gallon (about 4 L) oil

About 11 ounces (300 g) cod fillet

Juice of ½ lemon

DIRECTIONS

Prepare your fire for medium heat.

Place the fries in a large bowl and cover with water. Set aside while you prepare the remaining ingredients. (This removes excess starch, which helps the fries get extra crispy.) Drain well before frying.

To make the tartar sauce
In a medium bowl, combine the pickles, shallot, garlic, yogurt, mayonnaise, mustard, lemon juice, salt, pepper, and parsley. Mix well and taste for seasoning. Set aside. (It can safely sit out until the rest of the food is cooked, but if it's particularly hot outside, or you're at all concerned for food safety, put it your cooler—or make it after you cook the fish.)

To make the "mushy peas"
In a large cast-iron skillet over medium heat, combine the oil and butter. When the butter melts, add the peas and cook until they start to soften and take on color. Sprinkle with salt and pepper and stir in the mustard. Smash the peas in the skillet, remove the skillet from the heat, and cover to keep warm (the cast iron should retain its heat for a while).

Prepare your fire for high heat.

continued

To make the fish and chips

Place the flour in a large bowl and stir in the beer until a thin batter forms. Stir in the kale and spices.

Fill a large pot with the oil and set it over high heat. When hot (see Forest Hack, at left), carefully add the potatoes, in batches if necessary, and fry until deeply golden, 5 or 6 minutes. Use a slotted spoon or spider, or do like we do and use a branch, to carefully remove the fries from the hot oil.

Dip the fish in the beer batter, coating both sides. Allow excess batter to drip off and gently add the fish to the hot oil. Cook until deeply golden brown, 2 to 3 minutes.

Sprinkle salt over the fish and chips and give them a squeeze of lemon. Serve with the tartar sauce and mushy peas.

HERB-CRUSTED COD

The idea for this dish was to create pasta out of vegetables. It just sounded cool to us! We cut the veggies into long, very thin strips, but by all means, use a spiralizer, if you have one. We only used about half of each of the vegetables listed here, but you could easily put it all in the skillet. As for the fish, choose center-cut portions, for a nice square or rectangular slab. This ensures even cooking (and a better fit in the skillet).

INGREDIENTS

Scant 1 cup (100 g) dried bread crumbs

Large handful of fresh parsley, finely chopped, plus more for garnish

Handful of fresh basil, finely chopped

1 tablespoon (5.6 g) red pepper flakes

1 tablespoon (18 g) table salt, plus 1 teaspoon

1 tablespoon (6 g) black pepper, plus 1 teaspoon

2 large eggs, lightly beaten

¾ cup plus 1 heaping tablespoon (100 g) all-purpose flour

2 (6-ounce, or 170 g) cod fillets

6 tablespoons plus 2 teaspoons (100 ml) oil, divided

3 tablespoons plus 1 teaspoon (50 g) butter

4 garlic cloves, minced

¾ cup plus 1 tablespoon plus 1 teaspoon (200 ml) heavy cream

2 tablespoons (30 g) whole-grain mustard

Grated zest of 1 lemon

Grated zest of 1 lime

1 tablespoon (1.7 g) dried marjoram

1 carrot, cut into thin "noodles"

1 parsnip, peeled and cut into thin "noodles"

1 red onion, sliced

1 medium zucchini, cut into thin "noodles"

1 spring onion, sliced

½ cup (50 g) grated Parmesan cheese

DIRECTIONS

Prepare your fire for medium heat.

In a large bowl, combine the bread crumbs, parsley, basil, red pepper flakes, 1 tablespoon salt, and 1 tablespoon black pepper.

Set up a breading station with the eggs in a second bowl and the flour in a third bowl (or mounded on your cutting board).

Dredge each piece of fish in the flour, coating all sides, then dip it into the egg, allowing excess to drip off. Evenly coat the fish in the bread crumb mixture.

In a large cast-iron skillet over medium heat, combine 1 tablespoon oil and the butter. Add the garlic and cook until brown. Pour in the cream and stir in the mustard, lemon zest, lime zest, marjoram, remaining 1 teaspoon of salt, and remaining 1 teaspoon of pepper. Bring to a bubble and add the sliced vegetables. Cook until the vegetables are al dente, not more than 5 minutes, or the zucchini will disappear. Stir in the Parmesan and cook until melted and the flavors are blended. Remove the skillet from heat and transfer the vegetables to a platter or serving dish. Clean the skillet.

Return the clean skillet to medium heat and add the remaining 5 tablespoons plus 2 teaspoons of oil. When shimmering, add the coated fish and cook until a deep golden crust forms, about 3 minutes per side.

Spoon the veggie sauce over the fish and sprinkle with chopped parsley.

BURGERS, SANDWICHES, TACOS, AND QUESADILLAS

We get it. Not everyone wants to sit down and carve into a massive steak or go through the (very worthwhile) effort of making a stuffed-crust pizza in the forest. Sometimes, you want to eat sooner rather than later, with a bit less fuss. It's for these reasons that we include some of our favorite handhelds, including a massive double-decker cheeseburger, a giant taco in a crispy cheese shell, and a pita of shredded chicken that's bathed in a tangy sauce so amazing we really ought to bottle it. The one thing these sandwiches, etc., all have in common is that they are not meant for polite company!

CHICKEN FAJITAS

Tortillas are super simple to make in the forest and, we have to admit, they just taste better that way. You want to use a higher heat when cooking them to get that nice bubbly char; if you cook the tortillas longer over a lower heat, they'll get crispy—and we're not making tacos here. Lower the heat, though, when it comes time to cooking the filling.

INGREDIENTS

For the tortillas

½ cup plus 2 tablespoons (150 ml; plus or minus) water

1 thyme sprig, leaves stripped

1⅔ cups (200 g) all-purpose flour, plus more for dusting

1½ teaspoons baking powder

1 teaspoon table salt

2 tablespoons plus 2 teaspoons (40 ml) olive oil

For the filling

2 tablespoons (30 ml) olive oil

2 chicken breasts, cut lengthwise into strips

3 bell peppers, a mix of colors, cut into strips

1 red onion, halved and sliced

4 garlic cloves, sliced

1 tablespoon (18 g) table salt

1 tablespoon (6 g) ground black pepper

1 tablespoon (3 g) dried oregano

1 tablespoon (7 g) ground cumin

2 limes, ½ of 1 sliced, the second lime halved, rest reserved for juice

Chopped fresh parsley or cilantro for garnish

DIRECTIONS

Prepare your fire for high heat. (If using a grill, set up one side for high heat and one side for medium heat.)

To make the tortillas

Put your water and thyme leaves in a camp cup and set it next to your fire while you gather the remaining ingredients. (Or, put it in a small saucepan on the edge of your grill.) It'll be warm enough once you're ready to make your dough.

In a large bowl, stir together the flour, baking powder, and salt. Gradually add the warm water, along with the oil, stirring just until combined. Dump the dough onto a cutting board and knead until a smooth, pliable dough ball forms, 6 to 8 minutes.

Cut the dough into six pieces. Roll each piece into a ball, lightly flour the balls, then use a rolling pin to roll each into a very thin round, 7 or 8 inches (18 or 20 cm) in diameter. (They're thin enough if you can just about see your fingers through them.)

Put a large cast-iron skillet over high heat and place one tortilla in it. Cook until it bubbles and starts to char in places on the bottom, about 1 minute. Flip and cook the other side until golden, about 1 minute more. Remove from the heat and repeat with the remaining tortillas.

Prepare your fire for medium heat.

continued

BUSHCRAFT
Make Your Own Fajita Holders

When we made our first fajita, we tried filling it while holding the tortilla by hand. The filling got all over the place because we couldn't keep it steady. So, we thought, why not make a holder? It's something unusual that *we* haven't seen before, and we wondered, *What can we surprise people with*? Here's how to make your own:

1. Find four or six branches and cut off errant twigs, leaving you with a just "Y"-shaped fork at the end of each. The longer, bottom part of the "Y" should be long enough that part of it can go into the ground.

2. Whittle the two top branches of the "Y" clear of bark.

3. Stick them, in pairs, in the ground. Each pair should be close enough to comfortably hold a filled tortilla without it falling through the middle.

To make the fajitas

Pour the oil into the skillet and place it over medium heat. When shimmering, add the chicken and cook until lightly browned on all sides. Add the bell peppers, onion, and garlic and stir everything. Add the salt, pepper, oregano, and cumin and stir to coat. Place the lime slices on top and squeeze the juice from the remaining lime half into the skillet. Cook until the chicken is cooked through and the peppers are crisp-tender (you don't want them to be soggy), about 10 minutes.

Set the tortillas in holders and spoon in the filling. Garnish with chopped parsley and a squeeze of lime juice from the remaining lime halves.

CHICKEN QUESADILLAS WITH FOREST-MADE TORTILLAS

What you're going to notice straight away about this recipe is the mint-yogurt sauce. If we're honest, we weren't big fans of adding mint into sauce of any kind, but once we tried it with the quesadilla, it's been really hard to forget its refreshing taste. People like to go with the obvious (such as garlic and cumin), but we like to look at things differently. The mint and yogurt give something extra and add balance. It's nice to try, and we hope you will.

INGREDIENTS

For the sauce
3 garlic cloves, peeled

Handful of fresh mint leaves, torn

1 teaspoon table salt

1 teaspoon ground black pepper

¼ cup (60 g) plain yogurt

1 tablespoon (6 g) grated lime zest

For the chile tortillas
1⅔ cups (200 g) all-purpose flour, plus more for dusting

1½ teaspoons baking powder

1 teaspoon table salt

½ teaspoon ground black pepper

2 tablespoons (30 ml) olive oil

6 tablespoons plus 2 teaspoons (100 ml) warm water (see Forest Hack, page 181)

1 tablespoon (9 g) chopped fresh red chile

1 tablespoon (4 g) chopped fresh parsley

For the filling
2 tablespoons (30 ml) oil

2 chicken breasts, cut into ½-inch (1 cm) pieces

2 bell peppers, any color, diced

1 yellow onion, finely diced

1 teaspoon dried oregano

1 teaspoon sweet paprika

1 teaspoon table salt

1 teaspoon ground black pepper

Grated mozzarella cheese for serving

Chopped fresh parsley for garnish

DIRECTIONS

Prepare your fire for high heat. (If using a grill, set up one side for medium heat and one side for high heat.)

To make the sauce
Use a mortar and pestle to mash the garlic, mint, salt, and pepper into a paste. Stir in the yogurt and lime zest. (If you don't have a mortar and pestle, combine the ingredients in a food processor and pulse a few times.) Set aside.

To make the tortillas
In a large bowl, stir together the flour, baking powder, salt, and pepper. Pour in the oil and warm water and mix until a dough starts to come together. Add the chile and parsley and knead until a soft, pliable dough ball forms, 6 to 8 minutes.

Generously dust a cutting board with flour and put the dough on it. Cut the dough into six equal pieces. Use a rolling pin to roll one piece of dough into a very thin round, about 9 inches (23 cm) in diameter.

Place a large cast-iron skillet over high heat and add the tortilla. Cook until it bubbles all over and is browned in spots on the bottom, then flip, lightly browning the other side, about 1 minute per side. Repeat with the remaining dough.

Prepare your fire for medium heat.

continued

To make the filling
In a large cast-iron skillet over medium heat, heat the oil until it's shimmering. Add the chicken and cook until browned on all sides. Add the bell peppers, onion, and spices. Cook, stirring occasionally, until the chicken is cooked through and the peppers are crisp-tender, about 8 minutes. (It will smell as amazing as it looks at this point.) Transfer the filling to a bowl and carefully clean the skillet.

To assemble
Return the clean skillet to medium heat and place one cooked tortilla in it. Sprinkle a handful of mozzarella over the entire surface and top with a few spoonfuls of the chicken filling to cover. Sprinkle with a bit more cheese and top with a second tortilla. Cook both sides until golden and the cheese is melted, not longer than 5 minutes total. Repeat with the remaining ingredients.

To serve, quarter each quesadilla. Drizzle with the sauce and sprinkle with parsley.

FOREST HACK

Put your water in a camp cup and set it next to your fire while you gather your ingredients (or put it in a small saucepan and set it on the grill). It'll be warm enough once you're ready to make your tortilla dough.

SMOKED PORK BELLY SANDWICH

Always looking for a challenge, we thought we'd try ciabatta because we'd never made it before. It turned out pretty great, even if we scorched the tomatoes a bit. This is one of those recipes for which you'll want to concentrate your top coals around the edges of the lid when you bake the bread. But even if your bread does scorch, we promise you won't even notice once you sink your teeth into that pork belly slathered in its sweet-and-spicy beer-mustard sauce.

INGREDIENTS

For the ciabatta

2½ cups (300 g) all-purpose flour, plus more for dusting

1 tablespoon (12.5 g) sugar

1 tablespoon (3 g) dried oregano, plus more for sprinkling

Scant 2 teaspoons active dry or instant yeast

Table salt

6 tablespoons plus 2 teaspoons (100 ml) warm milk (see Forest Hack)

6 tablespoons plus 2 teaspoons (100 ml) warm water

1 tablespoons (15 ml) olive oil, plus more for drizzling

3 cocktail or cherry tomatoes, halved

1 garlic clove, sliced

For the pork

About 11 ounces (300 g) smoked pork belly, sliced ½ inch (1 cm) thick

1 small yellow onion, halved and sliced

3 garlic cloves, peeled

2 fresh chiles (1 red, 1 green), sliced (seeds retained for more heat)

1 (12-ounce, or 355 ml) bottle beer

3 tablespoons (60 g) honey

2 tablespoons (30 g) whole-grain mustard

3 tablespoons plus 1 teaspoon (50 ml) soy sauce

DIRECTIONS

Prepare your fire for low heat. (If using a grill, set up one side for low/indirect heat and one side for medium-high heat.)

To make the ciabatta
In a large bowl, stir together the flour, sugar, oregano, yeast, and 1 teaspoon salt. Add the warm milk, stirring it into the flour, then add the warm water and oil as more moisture is needed until all the flour is fully incorporated and you have a dry, craggy-looking dough ball (you might have to use your hands near the end). Knead until a stiff but pliable dough ball forms, 6 to 8 minutes. Cover the dough with an inverted bowl and set near the fire while you prepare the other ingredients for the bread. See "Where's the Rise," on page 139.

continued

FOREST HACK

Put your milk and water in camp cups and set them next to your fire while you gather your ingredients. (Or put them in saucepans on the grill.) They'll be warm enough once you're ready to make your dough.

Generously dust a cutting board with flour and place the dough on it. Stretch the dough, making sort of a rectangle, not quite the length of your board. Twist the dough a few times, then press into the twists to form a new rectangular loaf; it should now be just long enough to fit into your skillet. Press a few tomato halves into the top of the dough and sprinkle the sliced garlic over it. Drizzle with oil and sprinkle with a good pinch of salt and more oregano. Transfer to a large cast-iron skillet and place the skillet over low heat. Cover with an inverted skillet and place a large handful of coals on top (or close the grill lid). Cook until the top is nice and golden and the bread is cooked through, about 25 minutes, replenishing the coals as needed. Transfer the bread to a clean cutting board and carefully clean the skillet.

Prepare your fire for medium-high heat.

To make the pork
Return the clean skillet to medium-high heat and add the pork belly. Cook until beautifully golden on both sides, then scoot the pork to one side of the skillet. Add the onion and whole garlic. Cook until the vegetables start to brown and soften, then stir everything together. Add the chiles, beer, honey, mustard, and soy sauce. Stir to combine and cook until the sauce is reduced and jammy, 15 to 20 minutes.

Halve the ciabatta lengthwise and pile the pork mixture on the bottom half. Top with the other loaf half and halve the loaf to share.

MASSIVE STEAK SANDWICH

We made this bookmaker sandwich when we stopped for something to eat while out kayaking. It was a snowy, icy day, about 30°F (-1°C), and we decided to go on the lake. There was nothing crazy about it (at the time), and we could see maybe 100 yards or so (100 m) in front of us. But, as we cooked, the fog got thicker. We jumped back in the kayak and literally could see only 5 or 6 yards or so (5 or 6 m) in any direction. There was no joke about it because we didn't know which direction to go—and the lake was huge. And although the sandwich was very tasty (and filling), that was the last time we went kayaking in those conditions!

DIRECTIONS

Prepare your fire for medium-high and low heat (see How to Set Up Two-Zone Cooking with Your Campfire, page 187).

Drizzle the steaks with oil, rubbing it over both sides, then generously season with salt and pepper on all sides.

INGREDIENTS

2 sirloin steaks (1 inch, or 2.5 cm, thick)

Olive oil

Table salt

Ground black pepper

1 small yellow onion, halved and sliced

5⅓ ounces (150 g) white or brown mushrooms, sliced

Chopped fresh parsley for seasoning

1 tablespoon plus 2 teaspoons (25 g) butter, plus more for the ciabatta

4 garlic cloves, peeled

Few rosemary sprigs

Few thyme sprigs

1 loaf ciabatta, halved lengthwise

Place a griddle pan over medium-high heat and drizzle with a thin coat of oil. When shimmering, add the onion and cook until it starts to brown. Add the mushrooms and cook until well browned. Sprinkle with salt, pepper, and a handful of chopped parsley, stir to distribute, then scoot everything to the cool side.

continued

HOW TO SET UP TWO-ZONE COOKING WITH YOUR CAMPFIRE

Because we were making a pit stop, rather than spending the day in the forest, we wanted to keep the fire setup simple. We found a large flat log for the base (you could also use a large flat rock) and stacked large rocks on either side, making the stacks as stable as possible. The stacks should be high enough for a medium to medium-high fire underneath and just far enough apart to set the edges of the grill pan on them. (If the stacks are too high, you'll have to keep adding wood to the fire to keep the griddle smoking hot.) Start the fire as you normally would. Later, when it's time to cook the steaks while keeping the mushrooms warm, we moved almost all the coals underneath the steak side of the pan. You can do something similar with any campfire, so long as you have the space to pile your coals under one side of the pan.

Add a touch more oil to the pan and add the steaks to the hot side. Cook until a deep-brown crust develops, then flip. Add the butter to the skillet, placing it around the steaks, along with the garlic, rosemary, and thyme. Cook, periodically basting the steak with the butter and juices, until done to your liking, 2½ to 3 minutes per side. Transfer everything to a cutting board.

Butter the pan and place the bread in it, cut-side down. Cook until toasted, then flip. While the bread toasts, thickly slice the steaks crosswise.

Top one half of the bread with the mushroom mixture. Lay the steak slices on top of the mushrooms. Sprinkle with more parsley. Top with the other bread half. Halve the sandwich to share with your buddy.

DIRTY CHEESEBURGER

We swear you've never had a burger like this one. Why did we make it so massive? To be honest, people try to attract social media viewers with different things, and two small burgers would just be *two small burgers*, so we figured why not make one giant double burger? We're hungry fellas and even we couldn't finish it! And we call it a "dirty" cheeseburger because there's a lot of cheese, a lot of sauce, and it's very juicy. You're going to need extra napkins.

INGREDIENTS

For the burger bun

1 2/3 cups (200 g) all-purpose flour, plus more for dusting

1 tablespoon (12.5 g) sugar

Scant 2 teaspoons active dry or instant yeast

1 teaspoon table salt

3 tablespoons plus 1 teaspoon (50 ml) melted butter (see Forest Hack, page 190)

1 large egg

1/2 cup plus 2 tablespoons (150 ml) warm water

1 large egg yolk, beaten

Sesame seeds

For the sauce

1/4 small yellow onion, finely diced

1/2 teaspoon table salt

1/2 teaspoon ground black pepper

3 tablespoons (45 g) mayonnaise

1 tablespoon (16 g) tomato paste

1 tablespoon (15 g) English mustard (see page 116) or Dijon (but the flavor will be milder)

1 tablespoon (15 g) whole-grain mustard

3 Polish dill pickles, 1 finely diced, 2 sliced

For the burgers

1 2/3 pounds (750 g) ground beef

1 teaspoon table salt

1 teaspoon ground black pepper

1 teaspoon dried oregano

1/2 to 1 teaspoon red pepper flakes

Oil for frying

1 3/4 ounces (50 g) white cheddar cheese, sliced into thin planks

1 3/4 ounces (50 g) blue cheese, thinly sliced

Handful of chopped or shredded lettuce

DIRECTIONS

Prepare your fire for low heat. (If using a grill, set up one side for low/indirect heat and one side for medium heat.)

To make the bun

In a large bowl, stir together the flour, sugar, yeast, and salt. Add the melted butter and egg. Gradually stir while slowly pouring in the warm water until all the flour is fully incorporated and you have a dry, craggy-looking dough ball (you might have to use your hands near the end). Knead until a smooth, pliable dough ball forms, 6 to 8 minutes. Sprinkle with more flour, cover with another bowl, and set near the fire to rest while you prepare the remaining ingredients. See "Where's the Rise," on page 139.

continued

FOREST HACK

Put your water and butter in camp cups and set them next to your fire while you gather your ingredients. They'll be warm enough (and melted) once you're ready to make your dough.

Generously dust a cutting board with flour and place the dough on it. Give the dough a few kneads until a smooth dough ball forms, then place the dough in a large, well-seasoned cast-iron skillet over low heat. Brush/spoon the egg yolk over the top, sprinkle with sesame seeds, and cover with an inverted skillet. Top with a handful of coals (or close the grill lid) and cook until the top of the bun is deeply golden and the bun is cooked through, about 25 minutes. (For this you want the heat a little lower on top, so it doesn't burn the sesame seeds; you could also leave the center of the top skillet with fewer coals, concentrating them more around the edges; see page 129.) Meanwhile, make the sauce and prepare the burgers.

To make the sauce

Use a mortar and pestle to mash together the onion, salt, and pepper. Add the mayonnaise, tomato paste, English and whole-grain mustards, and diced pickle and stir well to thoroughly combine. (If you don't have a mortar and pestle, mince the onion first, then just combine the ingredients in a bowl and stir.)

To make the burgers

Prepare your fire for medium heat.

In a large bowl, mix the ground beef with the spices until well distributed. Divide the meat in half and form each half into a massive beef patty, a good 1 inch (2.5 cm) thick.

Pour a thin layer of oil into a large cast-iron skillet and place it over medium heat. When shimmering, add the patties (you might have to wedge them in to fit). Cook until deeply brown, about 4 minutes, then flip. Top one patty with the cheddar and the other with the blue cheese. Cover with an inverted skillet (no need for coals here; or close the grill lid) and cook until done to your liking, about 4 minutes more.

Slice the bun horizontally and slather the sauce on both halves. Top the bottom bun half with some lettuce, pickles slices, and burgers, then the top bun. Cut the whole shebang in half and have fun eating it. (We struggled to pick it up!)

BEST MEATBALL SANDWICH EVER

Good thing we're in the forest, because these sandwiches aren't built for high society! And what's more, we implore you to try this sauce with the anchovies. You won't be disappointed! It is one of the best tomato sauces we've ever encountered; in fact, ever since we made this sandwich, we always add anchovies to our tomato sauce. People think, *Fish?* If you never use them, that's fair; this recipe is just a guide. You're the one eating the food, so cook it for yourself. That said, if you want to experience something different, you have to try it. The anchovies are quite salty and they give you that nice, extra flavor. It's really beautiful.

INGREDIENTS

For the meatballs

About 1 pound, 2 ounces (500 g) ground beef

1 tablespoon (15 g) whole-grain mustard

1 teaspoon dried oregano

1 teaspoon table salt

1 teaspoon ground black pepper

1/2 to 1 teaspoon red pepper flakes

1 to 2 tablespoons (15 to 30 ml) oil

For the sauce

1 to 2 tablespoons (15 to 30 ml) olive oil

1 yellow onion, finely diced

4 garlic cloves, sliced

4 tomatoes, diced

3 tablespoons plus 1/2 teaspoon (50 g) tomato paste

5 oil-packed anchovy fillets

1 1/2 tablespoons (30 g) honey

1 teaspoon fresh thyme leaves

1 teaspoon dried oregano

1 teaspoon grated lemon zest

1 teaspoon table salt

1 teaspoon ground black pepper

2 balls fresh mozzarella, torn into thirds

Chopped fresh parsley for garnish

1 baguette

DIRECTIONS

Prepare your fire for medium heat. (If using a grill, set up one side for medium heat and one side for medium-low heat.)

continued

WHAT'S WITH ALL THE PARSLEY?

You might be wondering, *Why so much parsley everywhere*? We just happen to enjoy parsley and think it looks nice. And, if we don't add the parsley in our videos, people ask where it is. So, now you know. As always, do what you like—skip it or choose another herb for garnish.

To make the meatballs

In a large bowl, combine the ground beef, mustard, and spices. Mix with your hands until it all comes together. Form the meat mixture into balls somewhere between golf ball and tennis ball size (you'll want nine).

In a large cast-iron skillet over medium heat, heat the oil until it's shimmering. Carefully add the meatballs to the skillet and cook until deeply golden brown on all sides (they don't need to be cooked through at this point). Transfer the meatballs to a plate and carefully clean the skillet.

To make the sauce

Return the clean skillet to medium heat and pour in the oil. When shimmering, add the onion and cook until it just starts to brown and soften, then add the garlic and cook for 1 minute more until fragrant. Add the tomatoes and cook until they start to break down and bubble. Stir in the tomato paste and cook until the tomatoes are broken down and saucy. Add the anchovies, honey, thyme, oregano, lemon zest, salt, and pepper, stirring to combine. It's okay to let your fire burn down a bit, so as not to burn the sauce.

Nestle the meatballs into the sauce and nestle the torn mozzarella pieces among the meatballs. Cover with an inverted skillet and place a handful of coals on top (or close the grill lid). Cook until the sauce is thick, the cheese is melted, and the meatballs are cooked through, 5 to 10 minutes. Sprinkle with parsley.

Cut the baguette into thirds and cut each third in half horizontally (for three sandwiches). Scoop two pieces of cheese and some sauce onto each bottom piece of bread. Top with three meatballs, more sauce, and the top piece of bread before stuffing your face.

EPIC CHEESE TACO

Yes, this recipe makes one huge taco. We don't call it "epic" for nothing, and making your own taco shell out of cheese is half the fun! As for the guacamole, it is really all about personal taste. This recipe is just a guide; use as much or as little of each ingredient as tastes good to you.

INGREDIENTS

For the taco shell

1 cup (150 g) grated mozzarella

1 teaspoon ground black pepper

1 teaspoon paprika

1 teaspoon dried parsley

For the guacamole

1 avocado, peeled, halved, pitted, and chopped

¼ to ½ small red onion, finely diced

4 garlic cloves, chopped

⅔ cup (100 g) cocktail or cherry tomatoes, sliced

Juice of ½ to 1 lime, plus more as needed

½ teaspoon table salt, plus more as needed

½ teaspoon ground black pepper, plus more as needed

For the taco meat

About 1 pound, 2 ounces (500 g) ground beef

1 teaspoon paprika

1 teaspoon dried oregano

1 teaspoon garlic powder

1 teaspoon table salt

1 teaspoon ground black pepper

½ to 1 teaspoon cayenne pepper

Heaping ½ cup (150 g) tomato sauce

1 (12-ounce, or 355 ml) bottle beer

Chopped lettuce for serving

Diced red onion for serving

Sour cream for serving

Chopped fresh parsley or cilantro for garnish

DIRECTIONS

Prepare your fire for low heat. (If using a grill, set up one side for medium heat and one side for low/indirect heat.)

To make the taco shell

In a large bowl, stir together the mozzarella, black pepper, paprika, and parsley until the spices are well distributed.

Place a large cast-iron skillet over low heat and line it with parchment paper. Place two handfuls of cheese on the parchment, spreading it around to form a neat circle, almost to the edges of the skillet. Cover with an inverted skillet and place a handful of coals on top (or close the grill lid). Cook until the cheese melts and is golden, just a couple minutes. Immediately use the parchment paper to remove the shell from the skillet and, while it's still warm, lay it over a clean branch or the back of a clean chair, cheese-side down, and remove the paper. (We use the Noodle Drying Rack from page 28, but with a larger cross-branch to make the opening of the shell a little bigger.)

Prepare your fire for medium heat.

To make the guac

In a bowl, combine the avocado, onion, garlic, tomatoes, lime juice, salt, and black pepper, mashing the avocado as you go until everything is combined. Taste and adjust for seasoning. Set aside.

To make the taco meat
In a large cast-iron skillet over medium heat, cook the ground beef until no longer pink. Add the spices, stirring until the meat is coated. Stir in the tomato sauce, add the beer, and cook until the beer is evaporated, a few minutes.

Spoon the meat into the taco shell and top with guac, lettuce, onion, sour cream, and parsley. Share with a friend (or two).

BEST SHREDDED CHICKEN

Where we live, shredded pork is very popular. On the day we made this recipe, it was quite cold outside, about 25°F (-4°C). We had nothing better to do, and because we had never shredded *chicken* before, we thought, why not give it a shot and see how it goes? It was a long day out in the cold forest, but stuffing that hot shredded chicken into freshly made pitas was so worth it.

INGREDIENTS

For the pita dough

1 cup plus 2 teaspoons (250 ml) water

Scant 2 teaspoons active dry or instant yeast

1 teaspoon sugar

3⅓ cups (400 g) all-purpose flour, plus more for dusting

1 teaspoon table salt

Oil for frying

For the shredded chicken

1 tablespoon (15 ml) oil

1 tablespoon plus 1 teaspoon (20 g) butter

1 yellow onion, halved and sliced

3 garlic cloves, sliced

1-inch (2.5 cm) piece fresh ginger, peeled and very finely diced

2 (12-ounce, or 355 ml) bottles beer, divided

3 tablespoons plus ½ teaspoon (50 g) tomato paste

2 tablespoons plus 2 teaspoons (40 g) brown sugar

1 tablespoon plus 2 teaspoons (25 ml) teriyaki sauce

1 tablespoon plus 2 teaspoons (25 ml) soy sauce

1 tablespoon plus 1 teaspoon (20 g) whole-grain mustard

1 tablespoon plus 1 teaspoon (20 g) English mustard (see page 116) or Dijon (but the flavor will be milder)

1 teaspoon dried oregano

1 teaspoon red pepper flakes

1 teaspoon table salt

1 teaspoon ground black pepper

4 chicken breasts

Chopped fresh parsley for garnish

Sliced tomatoes for serving

Lettuce leaves for serving

DIRECTIONS

Prepare your fire for low heat. (If using a grill, set up one side for low/indirect heat and one side for medium heat.)

To make the pita

Warm the water in your camp cup near the fire (or a saucepan on the grill) and stir in the yeast and sugar, mixing until foamy. In a large bowl, stir together the flour and salt. Gradually pour in the water, mixing until a shaggy dough ball forms (you might need to use your hands near the end). Knead until a smooth, pliable dough ball forms, 6 to 8 minutes. Sprinkle with a little more flour, cover with an inverted bowl, and set the dough near the fire to rest while you prepare the remaining ingredients. See "Where's the Rise," on page 139.

Generously dust a cutting board with flour and put the dough on it. Cut the dough into quarters. Roll each piece to about 1/16 inch (0.16 cm) thick (it won't be quite the size of a 12-inch, or 30 cm, skillet).

Place a large cast-iron skillet over low heat and pour in a thin layer of oil. When hot, lay one piece of rolled-out dough in the bottom of the skillet and cover with a second inverted skillet. Top with a large handful of coals, covering almost the entire skillet (or close the grill lid), and cook until slightly puffed and golden, about 5 minutes, flipping once or twice. You might need to keep adding coals, depending on the conditions. Repeat with the remaining dough, adding more oil to the skillet as needed.

continued

Use a sharp knife to cut a 2-inch (5 cm) slit in the pita's edge and gently pull apart the edges to create a pocket. (Take care not to open it all the way like a book.)

Prepare your fire for medium heat.

To make the chicken
In a large cast-iron skillet over medium heat, combine the oil and butter. When the butter melts, add the onion, garlic, and ginger. Cook until the onion is golden and starts to soften.

Meanwhile, in a medium bowl, whisk one bottle of beer with the tomato paste, brown sugar, teriyaki and soy sauces, whole-grain and English mustards, and spices until well combined.

Lay the chicken on top of the cooking onion and pour the beer sauce over it. Pour the remaining bottle of beer around the chicken, taking care not to wash off the sauce on the chicken (it will bubble up). Cover with an inverted skillet (no need for coals here; or close the grill lid) and cook until the chicken is cooked through and the sauce is reduced and thickened, 40 to 45 minutes. (Basically, cook until it's ready and then leave it for 5 minutes longer, so you can easily shred it.) Remove from the heat.

Use two forks or knives to pull apart and shred the chicken while it's still in the skillet. Sprinkle with parsley and stir to coat the chicken with the sauce. Spoon the shredded chicken into a pita pocket lined with lettuce and tomato, and stuff it into your mouth.

THE FOREST BURGER

On the surface, this might seem like just any old hamburger. There's a sesame seed bun, and the burger's topped with cheese, lettuce, tomato, and onion. But, take a closer look. We add whole-grain mustard and Worcestershire sauce to the ground beef, along with paprika and oregano; we also skip the typical mayo in favor of a peppery, chive-y yogurt spread that's actually quite a nice accompaniment. And, of course, we cook it in the middle of the forest!

INGREDIENTS

For the burger bun

1²⁄₃ cups (200 g) all-purpose flour

1 tablespoon (12.5 g) sugar

Scant 2 teaspoons active dry or instant yeast

1 teaspoon table salt

2 tablespoons plus 2 teaspoons (40 g) butter, at room temperature

1 large egg

6 tablespoons plus 2 teaspoons (100 ml) water

Sesame seeds for garnish

For the sauce

4 garlic cloves, peeled

1½ teaspoons table salt, plus more as needed

½ to 1 teaspoon peppercorns

3 tablespoons (45 g) plain yogurt

1 tablespoon (3 g) chopped fresh chives

For the burgers

About 1 pound, 2 ounces (500 g) ground beef

1 tablespoon (3 g) dried oregano

1 tablespoon (8.4 g) paprika

1 tablespoon (18 g) table salt

1 tablespoon (6 g) ground black pepper

1 tablespoon (15 g) whole-grain mustard

1 tablespoon (15 ml) Worcestershire sauce

Oil for cooking

A few slices of cheese

Lettuce (leaves or sliced/shredded, as you prefer)

1 tomato, sliced

1 red onion, sliced

DIRECTIONS

Prepare your fire for low heat. (If using a grill, set up one side for low/indirect heat and one side for medium heat.)

To make the bun

In a large bowl, stir together the flour, sugar, yeast, and salt. Add the butter and egg, mixing until well dispersed. Gradually pour in the water, mixing until all the flour is fully incorporated and you have a dry, craggy-looking dough ball. Knead until a smooth, pliable dough ball forms, 6 to 8 minutes. Cover the dough with another bowl and set near the fire to rest while you prepare the remaining ingredients. See "Where's the Rise," on page 139.

continued

Place the dough in a large, well-seasoned cast-iron skillet over low heat. Sprinkle with sesame seeds, patting them into the dough, and cover with an inverted skillet. Top with a handful of coals (or close the grill lid) and cook until the top of the bun is deeply golden and the bun is cooked through, about 25 minutes. (For this you want the heat a little lower on top, so it doesn't burn the sesame seeds; you could also leave the center of the top skillet with fewer coals, concentrating them more around the edge; see page 129.) Meanwhile, make the sauce and prepare the burgers.

Prepare your fire for medium heat.

To make the sauce
Using a mortar and pestle, smash the garlic, salt, and peppercorns until you have a paste. Stir in the yogurt and chives. Taste for seasoning and set aside.

To make the burgers
In a large bowl, combine the ground beef, spices, mustard, and Worcestershire sauce, mixing until everything comes together. Divide the meat mixture into two equal portions and form each into a patty about the size of your palm.

In a large cast-iron skillet over medium heat, heat a thin layer of oil until its shimmering. Add the patties and cook until golden brown. Flip and top with your cheese of choice. Cook until done to your liking, 3 to 4 minutes more.

Slice the bun horizontally and schmear the bottom half with the sauce. Top with lettuce, the burgers, tomato, onion, and the top bun. Halve the burger to share.

RESOURCES

We've learned a lot of things during our outdoor adventures, but two things stand out:

1. The best cast-iron cookware you can afford really makes all the difference in your cooking.

2. If you want something done right, you have to do it yourself. That's where our **signature knife** comes in. Created by us and perfected by The Cooking Guild, it's available for sale at TheCookingGuild.com.

ACKNOWLEDGMENTS

Even though it is just the two of us out there in the forest, we could not have done this alone. We send a huge thank-you to our wives for all their support; our families have to put up with a lot! Thanks also to the team at the Quarto Group, particularly Thom O'Hearn; we weren't sure we wanted to go ahead with the book, but he convinced us we wouldn't have to sacrifice our time in the forest. To that point, thanks to Jennifer Kushnier, especially for her patience; we wouldn't change a word. Lastly, we'd like to thank our followers—without them, there'd be no reason to do any of this.

ABOUT THE AUTHORS

Slawek Kalkraut and Krzysztof Szymanski met ten years ago while working at different hotels on opposite sides of a lake. They decided to follow their passion for cooking and inspiring others (while still paying the bills) and launched *MenWithThePot* on Instagram in July 2019. Their playful, creative approach to food, their mesmerizing and appetizing videos, and the beauty of the countryside of Northern Ireland have since found millions of viewers across TikTok, Instagram, and YouTube. They live in County Fermanagh, Northern Ireland, with their families. When not in the forest, they can be found at MenWithThePot.com.

INDEX